DIABETIC COOKBOOK
FOR BEGINNERS:

SIMPLE AND DELICIOUS RECIPES FOR TYPE 2, PREDIABETES, AND NEWLY DIAGNOSED DIABETES. MASTER YOUR HEALTH WITH DELICIOUS LOW-CARB AND LOW-SUGAR MEALS

ANDREW FORESTRY

TABLE OF CONTENTS

1. INTRODUCTION TO DIABETES: EXPLANATION OF THE TYPES OF DIABETES, THE IMPORTANCE OF A HEALTHY DIET AND BLOOD GLUCOSE CONTROL 7
2. NUTRITION RECOMMENDATIONS FOR DIABETICS: ADVICE ON DIETARY COMPOSITION, PORTION SIZES, RATIONS, THE IMPORTANCE OF EATING COMPLEX CARBOHYDRATES AND NATURAL FOODS 9
3. BREAKFASTS 11
   - BLUEBERRY ALMOND OATMEAL 11
   - APPLE CINNAMON WALNUT OATMEAL 12
   - DIABETIC-FRIENDLY PEARL BARLEY PORRIDGE 13
   - QUINOA PORRIDGE 14
   - CREAMY BUCKWHEAT AND BERRY PORRIDGE 15
   - SPICED PEAR BUCKWHEAT PORRIDGE 16
   - SPINACH AND FETA OMELETTE 17
   - AVOCADO EGG WHITE SANDWICH 18
   - VEGGIE-PACKED EGG ROLLS 19
   - LIGHTENED-UP EGGS BENEDICT 20
   - CLASSIC DIABETIC-FRIENDLY EGG SALAD 21
   - CINNAMON APPLE MILLET PORRIDGE 22
   - MUSHROOM CUTLETS 23
4. SALADS 24
   - RADISH SALAD 24
   - SALAD WITH RADISH AND CARROTS 25
   - TANGY RADISH AND SPINACH SALAD 26
   - FRESH TOMATO AND CUCUMBER SALAD 27
   - TANGY CUCUMBER AND DILL SALAD 28
   - CRUNCHY ASIAN CABBAGE SALAD 29
   - EGG AND GREEN ONION SALAD 30
   - LEMON HERB MUSHROOM SALAD 31
   - BERRY CITRUS SALAD 32
5. GRAINS, LEGUMES, BEANS 33
   - CHICKPEA AND QUINOA PILAF 33

QUINOA AND BLACK BEAN SALAD	34
LENTIL AND BROWN RICE STUFFED BELL PEPPERS	35
THREE BEAN CHILI WITH QUINOA	36
CHICKPEA AND SPINACH CURRY	37
BLACK BEAN AND CORN SALSA WITH WHOLE GRAIN TORTILLA CHIPS	38
EDAMAME AND BARLEY SALAD	39
LENTIL AND VEGETABLE SOUP WITH BARLEY	40
BEAN AND FARRO BUDDHA BOWL	41
BLACK BEAN AND BROWN RICE BURRITO BOWL	42
6. BEEF, PORK AND LAMB	43
GRILLED FLANK STEAK WITH CHIMICHURRI	43
BEEF BRISKET	44
BEEF BOURGUIGNON	45
GRILLED SIRLOIN WITH MUSTARD RUB	46
BEEF STROGANOFF	47
BEEF WELLINGTON	48
BEEF POT ROAST	49
BEEF SHEPHERD'S PIE	50
BEEF CHILI	51
BEEF LASAGNA	52
BEEF TACOS	53
BEEF SHORT RIBS	54
PORK TENDERLOIN	55
PORK STIR-FRY	56
GRILLED PORK CHOPS	57
PULLED PORK (WITHOUT SUGARY SAUCES)	58
PORK LOIN ROAST	59
PORK CARNITAS (USING LEAN CUTS)	60
BAKED HAM	61
PORK AND VEGETABLES STIR-FRY	62
PORK AND BEAN SOUP	63
PORK STIR-FRY	64
PORK AND CABBAGE STIR-FRY	65

GRILLED LAMB CHOPS 66
HERB-CRUSTED LAMB RACK 67
LAMB KEBABS 68
LEMON GARLIC LAMB STEAKS 69
BRAISED LAMB SHANKS 70
GREEK-STYLE LAMB GYROS 71
ROAST LEG OF LAMB 72

7. POULTRY 73
   MEDITERRANEAN STUFFED CHICKEN BREAST 73
   CHICKEN AND VEGETABLE SKEWERS 74
   HERB-ROASTED TURKEY BREAST 75
   PARMESAN ALMOND CHICKEN CUTLETS 76
   HERB-CRUSTED BAKED CHICKEN BREAST 77
   MAPLE-GLAZED TURKEY TENDERLOIN 78
   LEMON GARLIC ROASTED CHICKEN THIGHS 79
   BAKED GOOSE LEGS WITH BAKED VEGETABLES 80
   FRIED GOOSE BREAST WITH BERRY SAUCE 81
   GRILLED QUAIL WITH CITRUS MARINADE 82

8. FISH AND SEAFOOD 83
   LEMON HERB BAKED COD 83
   DILL AND LEMON-POACHED TROUT 84
   STEAMED TILAPIA WITH LEMON AND HERBS 85
   SPICY PAPRIKA BAKED SALMON 86
   GINGER-POACHED TILAPIA 87
   STEAMED GINGER SOY HADDOCK 88
   GRILLED SHRIMP SKEWERS WITH VEGETABLE KABOBS 89
   SEAFOOD STIR-FRY 90
   STEAMED MUSSELS IN TOMATO AND HERB BROTH 91
   MUSSELS WITH GARLIC AND WHITE WINE SAUCE 92
   THAI-INSPIRED COCONUT CURRY MUSSELS 93
   BAKED LEMON-GARLIC SCALLOPS 94

9. STEWS AND SOUPS 95
   BEEF AND BARLEY STEW 95

- RABBIT STEW 96
- HEARTY VEGETABLE AND LENTIL STEW 97
- FISHERMAN'S STEW WITH COD AND VEGETABLES 98
- SPICY BLACK BEAN AND VEGETABLE STEW 99
- MOROCCAN CHICKPEA STEW 100
- CHICKEN AND VEGETABLE SOUP 101
- SPINACH AND WHITE BEAN SOUP 102
- MINESTRONE SOUP WITH WHOLE WHEAT PASTA 103
- MUSHROOM AND WILD RICE SOUP 104

10. SNACKS AND APPETIZERS 105
    - AVOCADO DEVILED EGGS FOR DIABETICS 105
    - VEGGIE STICKS WITH HUMMUS FOR DIABETICS 106
    - SMOKED SALMON CUCUMBER BITES FOR DIABETICS 107
    - CAPRESE SKEWERS WITH CHERRY TOMATOES 108
    - AND MOZZARELLA BALLS FOR DIABETICS 108
    - TUNA SALAD LETTUCE WRAPS FOR DIABETICS 109
    - SPICY EDAMAME FOR DIABETICS 110
    - HERB-ROASTED CHICKPEAS FOR DIABETICS 111

11. PIZZAS AND SANDWICHES 112
    - PORTOBELLO MUSHROOM CAP PIZZA WITH SPINACH AND FETA ... 112
    - WHOLE WHEAT VEGGIE PIZZA WITH CAULIFLOWER CRUST 113
    - BBQ CHICKEN PITA PIZZA WITH RED ONION AND BELL PEPPER 114
    - TURKEY AND AVOCADO SANDWICH ON WHOLE GRAIN BREAD 115
    - EGGPLANT PARMESAN SANDWICH ON WHOLE WHEAT CIABATTA .. 116
    - OPEN-FACED TUNA MELT ON WHOLE GRAIN ENGLISH MUFFIN 117
    - CAPRESE FLATBREAD WITH TOMATO, BASIL, AND FRESH MOZZARELLA 118
    - TURKEY AND CRANBERRY PANINI ON WHOLE GRAIN BREAD 119

12. DAIRY DISHES 120
    - LOW-FAT COTTAGE CHEESE AND TOMATO SALAD 120
    - GREEK YOGURT CHICKEN SALAD WITH APPLES AND ALMONDS ... 121
    - COTTAGE CHEESE PANCAKES WITH FRESH FRUIT 122
    - TOFU AND VEGETABLE STIR-FRY WITH SOY MILK SAUCE 123
    - RICOTTA AND SPINACH STUFFED MUSHROOMS 124

SKIM MILK OATMEAL WITH BERRIES 125
GREEK YOGURT RANCH DIP WITH VEGGIE STICKS 126
GREEK YOGURT BERRY PARFAIT WITH ALMOND GRANOLA 127
LOW-CARB CRUSTLESS QUICHE WITH BROCCOLI AND CHEDDAR 128
FETA AND SPINACH EGG MUFFINS 129

13. DESSERTS 130
BANANA NICE CREAM (FROZEN BANANA BLEND) 130
BAKED APPLES STUFFED WITH CINNAMON AND WALNUTS 131
SUGAR-FREE PUMPKIN PIE WITH A NUT CRUST 132
SUGAR-FREE BERRY CRISP WITH OAT TOPPING 133
ALMOND FLOUR BLUEBERRY MUFFINS 134
CHIA SEED PUDDING WITH UNSWEETENED ALMOND MILK 135
LOW-CARB CHEESECAKE WITH ALMOND FLOUR CRUST 136
DARK CHOCOLATE COVERED STRAWBERRIES 137
AVOCADO CHOCOLATE MOUSSE 138
NO-SUGAR-ADDED PEACH COBBLER WITH ALMOND FLOUR TOPPING 139
COCONUT FLOUR CHOCOLATE CHIP COOKIES 140
GREEK YOGURT PARFAIT WITH NUTS AND BERRIES 141

14. DRINKS 142
BERRY BLAST SMOOTHIE 142
GOLDEN MILK 143
GREEN SMOOTHIE 144
GINGER LEMONADE 145
TURMERIC LATTE 146
SPARKLING WATER WITH CITRUS AND FRESH HERBS 147
CUCUMBER MINT COOLER 148

CONCLUSIONS AND WISHES 149
ABOUT THE AUTHOR 150

1. INTRODUCTION TO DIABETES: EXPLANATION OF THE TYPES OF DIABETES, THE IMPORTANCE OF A HEALTHY DIET AND BLOOD GLUCOSE CONTROL

Introduction to Diabetes

Diabetes is a chronic health condition where the body struggles to manage blood sugar levels, either due to insufficient insulin production (Type 1) or insulin resistance (Type 2). It's a global health concern affecting millions of people worldwide. Managing diabetes involves careful monitoring of blood sugar, diet, exercise, and, in many cases, medication.

Types of Diabetes:

- Type 1 Diabetes: This autoimmune condition results in the body's immune system attacking insulin-producing cells in the pancreas. Individuals with Type 1 diabetes require daily insulin administration to maintain blood glucose levels.

- Type 2 Diabetes: Far more common, this form of diabetes is largely influenced by lifestyle factors and genetics. It's characterized by the body's inefficient use of insulin. Management includes lifestyle adjustments, oral medications, and sometimes insulin.

- Gestational Diabetes: This type affects some pregnant women and usually resolves after childbirth. However, it increases the risk of developing Type 2 diabetes later in life.

Importance of Healthy Eating

A balanced diet plays a critical role in managing diabetes and preventing Type 2 diabetes. Healthy eating helps stabilize blood sugar levels, maintain a healthy weight, and reduce the risk of diabetes-related complications. Key dietary considerations include reducing refined sugars, eating whole foods, and balancing macronutrients.

Blood Glucose Control

Maintaining blood glucose levels within a target range is crucial to prevent the short-term and long-term complications of diabetes. Strategies include regular monitoring of blood sugar levels, carbohydrate counting, and consistent medication adherence.

Conclusion

Understanding the types of diabetes and the significance of diet and blood glucose control is essential for management and prevention. By adopting healthy lifestyle choices, individuals can lead a fulfilling life despite diabetes. It's about making informed choices and taking proactive steps towards health and well-being.

2. NUTRITION RECOMMENDATIONS FOR DIABETICS: ADVICE ON DIETARY COMPOSITION, PORTION SIZES, RATIONS, THE IMPORTANCE OF EATING COMPLEX CARBOHYDRATES AND NATURAL FOODS

Introduction

Nutrition plays a pivotal role in managing diabetes, helping to maintain blood glucose levels within a target range, support overall health, and prevent complications. A well-planned diet can significantly impact a diabetic's quality of life.

Dietary Composition

For diabetics, a balanced intake of macronutrients is crucial:

- Carbohydrates: Choose complex carbohydrates over simple ones to ensure a slower release of glucose into the bloodstream.
- Proteins: Opt for lean sources of protein to support health without excessive saturated fats.
- Fats: Focus on healthy fats from sources like avocados, nuts, and olive oil, which can help manage cholesterol levels.

Portion Sizes and Rations

Understanding and controlling portion sizes are vital to managing calorie intake and blood sugar levels. Using measuring cups, scales, or visual comparisons (e.g., a fist equals a cup) can aid in keeping portions in check. Planning meals and snacks to ensure a balanced distribution of nutrients throughout the day is also important.

Complex Carbohydrates

Complex carbohydrates, found in whole grains, legumes, and vegetables, are essential for diabetics. They are digested more slowly, leading to a gradual increase in blood sugar levels, which helps in maintaining steady glucose levels. Incorporating complex carbohydrates into each meal is recommended.

Natural Foods

Emphasizing natural, whole foods over processed options benefits blood sugar control and overall health. Natural foods tend to be lower in added sugars and unhealthy fats. Fruits, vegetables, whole grains, and lean proteins should form the basis of a diabetic's diet.

Conclusion

Adhering to these nutrition recommendations can empower diabetics to manage their condition effectively. Focusing on dietary composition, portion control, complex carbohydrates, and natural foods can lead to better blood sugar control and a healthier life. It's about making informed, mindful choices every day.

3. BREAKFASTS

BLUEBERRY ALMOND OATMEAL

Yield: 4 servings | Prep time: 10 minutes | Cook time: 5 minutes

Ingredients:

2 cups water	1 cup fresh blueberries	4 tablespoons almond butter
1 cup steel-cut oats	1/4 cup sliced almonds	1/4 teaspoon salt
1/2 teaspoon cinnamon	2 tablespoons chia seeds	2 tablespoons maple syrup

Directions:

1. In a medium saucepan, bring water to a boil. Add the steel-cut oats and cinnamon, then reduce the heat to low. Simmer uncovered, stirring occasionally, until the oats are tender, about 5 minutes.

2. Remove from heat and stir in the almond butter, chia seeds, and salt. If using, sweeten with maple syrup.

3. Serve in bowls topped with fresh blueberries and sliced almonds.

Nutritional Information. Per serving: 295 calories, 10g protein, 38g carbohydrates, 14g fat, 9g fiber, 0mg cholesterol, 150mg sodium, 200mg potassium.

This recipe balances complex carbohydrates, healthy fats, and protein, making it an excellent choice for diabetics looking to maintain stable blood sugar levels. The addition of blueberries adds natural sweetness and antioxidants, while almond butter and chia seeds provide heart-healthy fats and additional fiber.

APPLE CINNAMON WALNUT OATMEAL

Yield: 4 servings | Prep time: 15 minutes | Cook time: 10 minutes

Ingredients:

2,5 cups water	1/2 teaspoon ground cinnamon	2 tablespoons ground flaxseed
1 cup old-fashioned rolled oats	1 medium apple, peeled and diced	4 teaspoons honey
1/4 cup walnuts, chopped		1/4 teaspoon salt

Directions:

1. In a large saucepan, bring water to a boil. Add the rolled oats, diced apple, and cinnamon, then reduce the heat to medium-low. Cook, stirring occasionally, until the oats are fully cooked and the mixture has thickened, about 10 minutes.

2. Remove from heat and stir in the ground flaxseed, walnuts, and salt. Sweeten with honey if desired.

3. Divide the oatmeal into bowls and serve warm, garnished with additional walnuts or a sprinkle of cinnamon if desired.

Nutritional Information. Per serving: 220 calories, 6g protein, 32g carbohydrates, 9g fat, 6g fiber, 0mg cholesterol, 160mg sodium, 150mg potassium.

This oatmeal recipe combines the heartiness of old-fashioned oats with the sweetness of apples and the crunch of walnuts, offering a delicious and nutritious breakfast option for diabetics. The addition of ground flaxseed not only boosts the fiber content, which is beneficial for blood sugar control, but also provides omega-3 fatty acids, contributing to heart health.

DIABETIC-FRIENDLY PEARL BARLEY PORRIDGE

Yield: 4 servings | Prep time: 10 minutes | Cook time: 40 minutes

Ingredients:

1 cup pearl barley, rinsed and drained	1/2 teaspoon cinnamon	1/4 teaspoon salt
4 cups water	1 tablespoon sugar-free maple syrup (or to taste)	1/4 cup chopped nuts (almonds, walnuts, or pecans)
1 cup unsweetened almond milk	1/2 cup fresh berries (blueberries, strawberries, etc.)	Optional: 1/2 teaspoon vanilla extract

Directions:

1. In a large saucepan, combine the pearl barley and water. Bring to a boil, then reduce heat to low, cover, and simmer for 30 minutes, or until the barley is tender and most of the water is absorbed.

2. Add the almond milk, cinnamon, salt, and optional vanilla extract to the saucepan with the barley. Cook for an additional 10 minutes, stirring occasionally, until creamy.

3. Remove from heat and stir in the sugar-free maple syrup. Adjust sweetness to taste.

4. Serve warm, topped with fresh berries and chopped nuts.

Nutritional Information. Per serving: 220 calories, 6g protein, 44g carbohydrates, 4g fat, 9g fiber, 0mg cholesterol, 80mg sodium, 250mg potassium per serving.

This pearl barley porridge is a hearty, nutritious option for diabetics, offering a good balance of complex carbohydrates, protein, and fiber to help manage blood sugar levels. The high fiber content in pearl barley helps slow down glucose absorption, making it an excellent choice for a diabetic-friendly breakfast or snack.

QUINOA PORRIDGE

Yield: 4 servings | Prep time: 10 minutes | Cook time: 20 minutes

Ingredients:

1 cup quinoa, rinsed 2 cups unsweetened almond milk 1/4 teaspoon nutmeg	1/2 teaspoon ground cinnamon 1 tablespoon sugar-free maple syrup (or to taste)	1/2 cup fresh blueberries 1/4 cup chopped nuts (almonds or walnuts) 1 teaspoon vanilla extract

Directions:

1. Combine the quinoa, almond milk, cinnamon, and nutmeg in a medium saucepan. Bring to a boil over medium-high heat. Then, reduce the heat to low, cover, and simmer for 15 minutes, or until most of the liquid is absorbed.

2. Remove from heat and stir in the sugar-free maple syrup and optional vanilla extract. Let it stand covered for 5 minutes; the quinoa will become fluffy and absorb the remaining liquid.

3. Serve warm, topped with fresh blueberries and chopped nuts.

Nutritional Information: Per serving: 210 calories, 8g protein, 32g carbohydrates, 7g fat, 5g fiber, 0mg cholesterol, 30mg sodium, 400mg potassium per serving.

This quinoa porridge recipe is particularly beneficial for individuals managing diabetes, offering a nutritious start to the day without spiking blood sugar levels. Quinoa is a high-fiber, high-protein grain, which contributes to its low glycemic index. This means it releases glucose slowly into the bloodstream, helping maintain stable blood sugar levels, a crucial aspect of diabetes management. The inclusion of unsweetened almond milk instead of regular dairy reduces the calorie and carbohydrate content, further supporting blood sugar control. The antioxidants found in blueberries and the healthy fats from nuts add to the nutritional profile of the meal, providing essential vitamins, minerals, and heart-healthy fats.

CREAMY BUCKWHEAT AND BERRY PORRIDGE

Yield: 4 servings | Prep time: 5 minutes | Cook time: 15 minutes

Ingredients:

1 cup buckwheat groats	1/2 teaspoon cinnamon	2 tablespoons ground flaxseeds
3 cups almond milk	1 cup mixed berries	
1 teaspoon vanilla extract	4 teaspoons agave syrup	1/4 teaspoon salt

Directions:

1. Rinse the buckwheat groats under cold water. In a medium saucepan, combine the buckwheat, almond milk, vanilla extract, and cinnamon. Bring to a boil, then reduce the heat to low and simmer, covered, stirring occasionally, until the buckwheat is tender and the mixture has thickened, about 15 minutes.

2. Remove from heat and stir in the salt and ground flaxseeds. Sweeten with agave syrup if desired.

3. Serve the porridge in bowls topped with mixed berries.

Nutritional Information. Per serving: 230 calories, 6g protein, 42g carbohydrates, 3g fat, 7g fiber, 0mg cholesterol, 160mg sodium, 300mg potassium.

This buckwheat porridge recipe offers a warm, nutritious, and comforting meal, perfect for diabetics seeking a balanced breakfast. Buckwheat, a highly nutritious whole grain, provides a good source of protein and fiber, which are essential for blood sugar control. The addition of berries not only adds natural sweetness and flavor but also boosts the meal's antioxidant content.

SPICED PEAR BUCKWHEAT PORRIDGE

Yield: 4 servings | Prep time: 10 minutes | Cook time: 20 minutes

Ingredients:

1 cup buckwheat groats	1/2 teaspoon ground ginger	2 tablespoons hemp seeds
3.5 cups water	1/2 teaspoon ground cinnamon	4 teaspoons maple syrup
1 large pear, diced	1/4 cup pecans, chopped	1/4 teaspoon salt

Directions:

1. Rinse the buckwheat groats under cold water. In a medium saucepan, combine the buckwheat, water, diced pear, ginger, and cinnamon. Bring to a boil, then reduce the heat to low and simmer, covered, stirring occasionally, until the buckwheat is tender and the porridge has thickened, about 20 minutes.

2. Remove from heat and stir in the salt. Sweeten with maple syrup if desired.

3. Serve the porridge in bowls, garnished with chopped pecans and a sprinkle of hemp seeds.

Nutritional Information. Per serving: 245 calories, 7g protein, 44g carbohydrates, 5g fat, 8g fiber, 0mg cholesterol, 150mg sodium, 350mg potassium.

This buckwheat porridge variation incorporates the gentle sweetness of pears with the warmth of ginger and cinnamon, offering a comforting and nutritious breakfast choice for diabetics. The addition of pecans and hemp seeds not only provides a satisfying crunch but also adds healthy fats and additional protein, making it a balanced meal that supports stable blood sugar levels.

SPINACH AND FETA OMELETTE

Yield: 2 servings | Prep time: 5 minutes | Cook time: 10 minutes

Ingredients:

4 large eggs	1 cup fresh spinach, chopped	1/4 teaspoon salt
1/4 cup almond milk		1/4 teaspoon black pepper
1/4 cup feta cheese, crumbled	1/2 medium tomato, diced	1 tablespoon olive oil

Directions:

1. In a medium bowl, whisk together the eggs, almond milk, salt, and pepper until well combined.

2. Heat the olive oil in a non-stick skillet over medium heat. Add the spinach and tomato, sautéing until the spinach is wilted, about 2 minutes.

3. Pour the egg mixture over the spinach and tomatoes in the skillet. Cook for about 4 minutes, or until the eggs are set on the bottom. Sprinkle the feta cheese over one half of the omelette.

4. Carefully fold the omelette in half and continue to cook for another 2 minutes or until the cheese is melted and the eggs are fully set.

Nutritional Information. Per serving: 290 calories, 20g protein, 4g carbohydrates, 22g fat, 1g fiber, 372mg cholesterol, 710mg sodium, 300mg potassium.

This Spinach and Feta Omelette is a flavorful and nutritious option for diabetics, offering a good balance of protein and healthy fats, with low carbohydrates. The addition of spinach and tomato not only enhances the flavor but also provides essential vitamins, minerals, and fiber, making it a satisfying meal to start the day.

AVOCADO EGG WHITE SANDWICH

Yield: 2 servings | Prep time: 5 minutes | Cook time: 5 minutes

Ingredients:

4 egg whites 2 whole wheat English muffins, split and toasted	1 ripe avocado, mashed 1 tomato, sliced 1/4 teaspoon salt	1/4 teaspoon black pepper 1 teaspoon olive oil

Directions:

1. Heat the olive oil in a non-stick skillet over medium heat. Season the egg whites with salt and pepper, then pour into the skillet, cooking until the whites are fully set, about 2-3 minutes per side.

2. Spread the mashed avocado onto each half of the toasted English muffins. Place a slice of tomato on the bottom halves.

3. Place the cooked egg whites on top of the tomato slices, then cover with the top halves of the English muffins to form sandwiches.

Nutritional Information. Per serving: 320 calories, 19g protein, 35g carbohydrates, 13g fat, 9g fiber, 0mg cholesterol, 620mg sodium, 600mg potassium.

This Avocado Egg White Sandwich offers a heart-healthy, diabetes-friendly breakfast option that's high in protein and fiber but low in cholesterol and saturated fat. The whole wheat English muffins provide complex carbohydrates for energy, while the avocado adds creamy texture and healthy fats. Tomato slices add freshness and a hint of sweetness, making this sandwich a balanced and nutritious choice for anyone managing diabetes.

VEGGIE-PACKED EGG ROLLS

Yield: 4 servings | Prep time: 15 minutes | Cook time: 10 minutes

Ingredients:

8 large eggs 1/2 cup bell peppers, finely diced 2 tablespoons olive oil	1/2 cup spinach, finely chopped 1/4 cup onions, finely diced	1/4 teaspoon salt 1/4 teaspoon black pepper 4 whole wheat tortillas

Directions:

1. In a large bowl, whisk together the eggs, salt, and pepper. Stir in the bell peppers, spinach, and onions until well combined.

2. Heat a tablespoon of olive oil in a non-stick skillet over medium heat. Pour in half of the egg mixture, tilting the pan to spread it out thinly. Cook for 2-3 minutes, or until the egg is set, then carefully flip and cook for another 1-2 minutes. Remove from the skillet and repeat with the remaining egg mixture and oil.

3. Place each cooked egg "sheet" on a whole wheat tortilla. Roll up tightly, then cut in half to serve.

Nutritional Information. Per serving: 330 calories, 20g protein, 24g carbohydrates, 18g fat, 4g fiber, 372mg cholesterol, 480mg sodium, 300mg potassium.

These Veggie-Packed Egg Rolls are a nutritious and delicious meal option for diabetics, combining the health benefits of vegetables with the protein-rich goodness of eggs. Wrapped in whole wheat tortillas, they offer a balanced combination of fiber, vitamins, and minerals, making them an excellent choice for a filling breakfast or a light lunch.

LIGHTENED-UP EGGS BENEDICT

Yield: 4 servings | Prep time: 20 minutes | Cook time: 10 minutes

Ingredients:

4 large eggs	1 cup baby spinach	1 teaspoon Dijon mustard
2 whole wheat English muffins, split and toasted	For the hollandaise sauce:	1/4 cup Greek yogurt
	2 egg yolks	1/4 teaspoon salt
4 slices of turkey bacon	1 tablespoon lemon juice	Dash of cayenne pepper

Directions:

1. To make the hollandaise sauce, whisk together egg yolks, lemon juice, and Dijon mustard in a heatproof bowl. Place the bowl over a pot of simmering water (double boiler method), whisking constantly until the mixture thickens. Remove from heat and whisk in Greek yogurt, salt, and cayenne pepper. Set aside.

2. In a skillet, cook the turkey bacon until crisp. Set aside. In the same skillet, quickly wilt the baby spinach, then remove from heat.

3. Poach the eggs in simmering water until the whites are set but the yolks are still runny, about 3-4 minutes.

4. Assemble the Eggs Benedict by placing half an English muffin on each plate, topped with turkey bacon, wilted spinach, a poached egg, and a drizzle of the hollandaise sauce.

Nutritional Information. Per serving: 250 calories, 19g protein, 22g carbohydrates, 11g fat, 3g fiber, 372mg cholesterol, 580mg sodium, 300mg potassium.

This Lightened-Up Eggs Benedict recipe offers a healthier twist on the classic, incorporating whole wheat English muffins, turkey bacon, and a Greek yogurt-based hollandaise sauce. It's a nutritious and satisfying option for diabetics, balancing protein, healthy fats, and fiber for a well-rounded breakfast or brunch.

CLASSIC DIABETIC-FRIENDLY EGG SALAD

Yield: 4 servings | Prep time: 10 minutes | Cook time: 0 minutes (Assuming eggs are pre-cooked)

Ingredients:

8 large eggs, hard-boiled and chopped	1/4 cup celery, finely chopped	1/4 cup red onion, finely chopped
1/4 cup Greek yogurt	1 tablespoon fresh dill, chopped (or 1 teaspoon dried dill)	Salt and pepper to taste
2 tablespoons mayonnaise		Lettuce leaves for serving (optional)
1 teaspoon Dijon mustard		

Directions:

1. In a large bowl, mix together the Greek yogurt, mayonnaise, and Dijon mustard until smooth.

2. Add the chopped eggs, celery, red onion, and dill to the bowl. Gently fold the ingredients together until the eggs are well coated with the dressing. Season with salt and pepper to taste.

3. Cover and chill in the refrigerator for at least 30 minutes to allow the flavors to meld.

4. Serve the egg salad on a bed of lettuce leaves or as a filling for a whole wheat sandwich or wrap.

Nutritional Information. Per serving: 210 calories, 13g protein, 3g carbohydrates, 16g fat, 0g fiber, 372mg cholesterol, 320mg sodium, 180mg potassium.

This Classic Diabetic-Friendly Egg Salad combines the creamy texture of Greek yogurt with the richness of mayonnaise and the tanginess of Dijon mustard, creating a healthy and flavorful option that's perfect for diabetics. The addition of celery and red onion provides a crunch and a burst of flavor, making this egg salad both nutritious and satisfying.

CINNAMON APPLE MILLET PORRIDGE

Yield: 4 servings | Prep time: 5 minutes | Cook time: 25 minutes

Ingredients:

1 cup millet 3 cups water 1 cup unsweetened almond milk	1 large apple, peeled and diced 2 teaspoons cinnamon 1 teaspoon vanilla extract	1 tablespoon sugar substitute (suitable for diabetics) A pinch of salt

Directions:

1. Rinse the millet under cold water until the water runs clear. In a medium saucepan, bring the water to a boil. Add the millet and a pinch of salt, reduce heat to low, cover, and simmer for 15 minutes.

2. Stir in the almond milk, diced apple, cinnamon, vanilla extract, and sugar substitute. Continue to cook for another 10 minutes, or until the porridge is creamy and the apples are tender.

3. Remove from heat and let it sit covered for 5 minutes. The porridge will thicken as it cools.

4. Serve warm, adding more almond milk if needed for desired consistency. Garnish with additional cinnamon or diced apple if desired.

Nutritional Information. Per serving: 235 calories, 6g protein, 45g carbohydrates, 3g fat, 5g fiber, 0mg cholesterol, 80mg sodium, 220mg potassium.

This Cinnamon Apple Millet Porridge is a comforting and diabetic-friendly breakfast option. The natural sweetness of the apple and the warmth of the cinnamon make this dish flavorful without the need for added sugars. Millet, a gluten-free grain, offers a hearty base that's high in fiber and protein, aiding in blood sugar control and providing a sustained energy source. This porridge is an excellent way to start the day, offering a nutritious and satisfying meal that aligns with a diabetic diet.

MUSHROOM CUTLETS

Yield: 4 servings | Prep time: 15 minutes | Cook time: 20 minutes

Ingredients:

1 lb ground turkey 1 cup finely chopped mushrooms 1/2 cup almond flour	1 small onion (finely chopped) 2 cloves garlic, minced 1 egg	2 tablespoons low-sodium soy sauce Salt and pepper to taste Olive oil for frying

Directions:

1. In a large bowl, combine ground turkey, chopped mushrooms, almond flour, onion, garlic, egg, soy sauce, salt, and pepper. Mix well until evenly combined.
2. Shape the mixture into patties, about 1/2 inch thick.
3. Heat olive oil in a skillet over medium heat. Add the patties and cook for about 5-7 minutes on each side, or until golden brown and cooked through.
4. Serve hot with steamed vegetables or a salad.

Nutritional Information. Per serving: 230 calories, 20g protein, 8g carbohydrates, 14g fat, 2g fiber, 85mg cholesterol, 350mg sodium, 280mg potassium.

This recipe for Mushroom Cutlets offers a healthy and delicious option for a meal, perfectly suited for those looking for a nutritious dish that doesn't skimp on flavor. This dish combines ground turkey and finely chopped mushrooms with almond flour, providing a low-carb and gluten-free alternative to traditional cutlets. The addition of onion, garlic, and low-sodium soy sauce adds depth to the flavor profile, while an egg helps bind the ingredients together. These cutlets are a great source of protein and can be served with a side of steamed vegetables or salad for a complete meal. This dish is not only delicious but also conducive to a healthy lifestyle, including those managing dietary restrictions or watching their intake of carbs and fats.

4. SALADS

RADISH SALAD

Yield: 4 servings | Prep time: 10 minutes | Cook time: 0 minutes

Ingredients:

| 2 cups sliced radishes | 1/4 cup chopped fresh parsley | 1 tablespoon lemon juice |
| 1/4 cup diced red onion | 2 tablespoons olive oil | Salt and pepper to taste |

Directions:

1. In a large bowl, combine the sliced radishes, diced red onion, and chopped parsley.
2. In a small bowl, whisk together the olive oil and lemon juice to make the dressing.
3. Pour the dressing over the radish mixture and toss until well-coated.
4. Season with salt and pepper to taste.
5. Serve immediately or refrigerate until ready to serve.

Nutritional Information. Per serving: 60 calories, 1g protein, 4g carbohydrates, 5g fat, 2g fiber, 0mg cholesterol, 150mg sodium, 250mg potassium.

The Radish Salad recipe is a crisp, refreshing dish perfect for those seeking a light and nutritious option. This easy salad combines the peppery bite of sliced radishes with the sharpness of red onion and the freshness of parsley. Dressed simply with olive oil and lemon juice, it offers a clean, zesty flavor that complements the radishes well. This salad is seasoned with just the right amount of salt and pepper, enhancing its natural tastes without overpowering them.

SALAD WITH RADISH AND CARROTS

Yield: 4 servings | Prep time: 15 minutes | Cook time: 0 minutes

Ingredients:

1 cup thinly sliced radishes	2 tablespoons chopped fresh parsley	2 tablespoons apple cider vinegar
1/2 cup shredded carrots	1 tablespoon sesame seeds	1 teaspoon honey (can be omitted for stricter diets)
1/4 cup diced cucumbers	Salt and pepper to taste	
1 tablespoon olive oil		

Directions:

1. In a large bowl, combine the sliced radishes, shredded carrots, diced cucumbers, and chopped parsley.

2. In a small bowl, whisk together the olive oil, apple cider vinegar, and honey (if using) until well combined. Season with salt and pepper to taste.

3. Pour the dressing over the salad and toss well to coat all the ingredients evenly.

4. Sprinkle sesame seeds over the salad before serving.

Nutritional Information. Per serving: 70 calories, 1g protein, 8g carbohydrates, 4g fat, 2g fiber, 0mg cholesterol, 30mg sodium, 200mg potassium.

This recipe offers a refreshing, low-calorie salad with a good balance of flavors and nutrients, making it suitable for diabetics and those looking to maintain a healthy diet.

TANGY RADISH AND SPINACH SALAD

Yield: 4 servings | Prep time: 15 minutes | Cook time: 0 minutes

Ingredients:

2 cups radishes, thinly sliced	1/4 cup feta cheese, crumbled	1/2 teaspoon salt
2 cups baby spinach leaves	1 tablespoon lemon juice	1/4 teaspoon black pepper
1/4 cup red onion, thinly sliced	1 teaspoon Dijon mustard	1 tablespoon fresh parsley, chopped
2 tablespoons olive oil		

Directions:

1. In a large salad bowl, combine the sliced radishes, baby spinach, and red onion.
2. In a small bowl, whisk together the olive oil, lemon juice, Dijon mustard, salt, and pepper to create the dressing.
3. Drizzle the dressing over the salad and toss gently to coat. Sprinkle with crumbled feta cheese and fresh parsley before serving.

Nutritional Information. Per serving: 110 calories, 3g protein, 4g carbohydrates, 9g fat, 2g fiber, 15mg cholesterol, 410mg sodium, 360mg potassium.

This salad offers a nutritious blend of vegetables, healthy fats, and a modest amount of protein, making it ideal for those managing diabetes. The radishes and spinach provide fiber and potassium, important for overall health, while the dressing adds a tangy flavor without adding excessive carbohydrates.

FRESH TOMATO AND CUCUMBER SALAD

Yield: 4 servings | Prep time: 15 minutes | Cook time: 0 minutes

Ingredients:

4 large ripe tomatoes, chopped	1/4 cup red onion, thinly sliced	2 tablespoons olive oil
1 large cucumber, peeled and chopped	1 tablespoon balsamic vinegar	1/4 cup fresh basil leaves, chopped
		Salt and pepper to taste

Directions:

1. In a large bowl, combine the chopped tomatoes, cucumber, and red onion.

2. Drizzle the olive oil and balsamic vinegar over the salad. Gently toss to coat the vegetables.

3. Season the salad with salt and pepper to taste. Sprinkle the chopped basil over the top just before serving.

4. Serve immediately or chill in the refrigerator for 30 minutes to allow the flavors to meld.

Nutritional Information. Per serving: 110 calories, 2g protein, 9g carbohydrates, 7g fat, 2g fiber, 0mg cholesterol, 10mg sodium, 400mg potassium.

This Fresh Tomato and Cucumber Salad is a vibrant, nutrient-rich dish perfect for diabetics looking for a low-calorie, flavorful side dish. The combination of fresh vegetables with the tanginess of balsamic vinegar and the richness of olive oil makes for a refreshing salad suitable for any meal. The addition of basil provides a fresh, herbal note that elevates the overall taste of the dish.

TANGY CUCUMBER AND DILL SALAD

Yield: 4 servings | Prep time: 10 minutes | Cook time: 0 minutes

Ingredients:

2 large cucumbers, thinly sliced	2 tablespoons olive oil	1 teaspoon honey (optional, adjust for diabetic diet)
1/4 cup red onion, thinly sliced	1 tablespoon fresh dill, chopped	Salt and pepper to taste
1/4 cup apple cider vinegar		

Directions:

1. In a large bowl, combine the thinly sliced cucumbers and red onion.

2. In a small bowl, whisk together the apple cider vinegar, olive oil, dill, and honey (if using) until well combined. Season with salt and pepper to taste.

3. Pour the dressing over the cucumber and onion slices. Toss gently to ensure all slices are evenly coated with the dressing.

4. Refrigerate for at least 30 minutes before serving to allow the flavors to meld together.

Nutritional Information. Per serving: 90 calories, 1g protein, 4g carbohydrates, 7g fat, 1g fiber, 0mg cholesterol, 2mg sodium, 180mg potassium.

This Tangy Cucumber and Dill Salad is a light and refreshing dish, perfect for diabetics seeking a flavorful yet low-calorie side. The apple cider vinegar and dill provide a sharp, tangy taste that complements the crispness of the cucumbers, while the olive oil adds a subtle richness. This salad is an excellent choice for a healthy, diabetic-friendly meal or side dish.

CRUNCHY ASIAN CABBAGE SALAD

Yield: 4 servings | Prep time: 15 minutes | Cook time: 0 minutes

Ingredients:

4 cups shredded cabbage	3 tablespoons rice vinegar	1 teaspoon grated ginger
1 large carrot, julienned	2 tablespoons sesame oil	1 garlic clove, minced
1/4 cup sliced green onions	1 tablespoon soy sauce	1 teaspoon sugar substitute
1/4 cup almonds, toasted	(low sodium)	(suitable for diabetics)

Directions:

1. In a large salad bowl, combine the shredded cabbage, julienned carrot, and sliced green onions.

2. In a small bowl, whisk together the rice vinegar, sesame oil, soy sauce, grated ginger, minced garlic, and sugar substitute to create the dressing.

3. Pour the dressing over the cabbage mixture and toss well to coat evenly.

4. Sprinkle the toasted slivered almonds over the salad just before serving.

Nutritional Information. Per serving: 120 calories, 3g protein, 8g carbohydrates, 9g fat, 3g fiber, 0mg cholesterol, 200mg sodium, 250mg potassium.

This Crunchy Asian Cabbage Salad is a vibrant and flavorful option for diabetics, featuring a colorful mix of vegetables and a tangy, low-sodium dressing. It's rich in vitamins and fiber, with a satisfying crunch from the almonds, making it an excellent side dish or light meal that supports blood sugar management.

EGG AND GREEN ONION SALAD

Yield: 4 servings | Prep time: 10 minutes | Cook time: 10 minutes

Ingredients:

6 large eggs	1 teaspoon Dijon mustard	3 green onions, thinly sliced
2 tablespoons olive oil	1/2 teaspoon salt	1 tablespoon chopped fresh
1 tablespoon white vinegar	1/4 teaspoon black pepper	parsley for garnish

Directions:

1. Place eggs in a large saucepan and cover with cold water by 1 inch. Bring to a boil over medium-high heat, then cover, remove from heat, and let stand for 9 minutes. After 9 minutes, transfer eggs to a bowl of ice water to cool.

2. Peel and chop the eggs. Whisk together olive oil, white vinegar, Dijon mustard, salt, and black pepper in a large bowl. Add the chopped eggs and sliced green onions to the bowl, and gently fold to combine.

3. Refrigerate the salad for at least 30 minutes before serving to allow flavors to meld. Serve chilled, garnished with fresh parsley if desired.

Nutritional Information. Per serving: 155 calories, 11g protein, 2g carbohydrates, 11g fat, 0g fiber, 372mg cholesterol, 410mg sodium, 126mg potassium.

This egg and green onion salad provides a high-protein, low-carbohydrate option suitable for diabetics, focusing on healthy fats from olive oil and nutrient-rich eggs. The low carbohydrate content helps manage blood sugar levels, making it an excellent choice for a diabetic-friendly meal or side dish.

LEMON HERB MUSHROOM SALAD

Yield: 4 servings | Prep time: 10 minutes | Cook time: 0 minutes

Ingredients:

3 cups mixed mushrooms (such as button, shiitake), thinly sliced	1/4 cup chives, finely chopped	1 garlic clove, minced
1/4 cup parsley, finely chopped	2 tablespoons olive oil	Salt and pepper to taste
	2 tablespoons lemon juice	1/4 cup shaved Parmesan cheese

Directions:

1. In a large bowl, combine the sliced mushrooms, parsley, and chives.
2. In a small bowl, whisk together the olive oil, lemon juice, minced garlic, salt, and pepper to create the dressing.
3. Pour the dressing over the mushroom mixture and toss gently to ensure all the mushrooms are coated.
4. If using, sprinkle the shaved Parmesan cheese over the salad before serving.

Nutritional Information. Per serving: 100 calories, 3g protein, 4g carbohydrates, 7g fat, 1g fiber, 4mg cholesterol, 75mg sodium, 300mg potassium.

This Lemon Herb Mushroom Salad is a fresh and light option ideal for diabetics, featuring a flavorful combination of herbs and lemon dressing that complements the earthiness of the mushrooms. The addition of Parmesan cheese adds a savory depth, but can be omitted for a lighter version. This salad is perfect for a nutritious side dish or a healthy snack that won't spike blood sugar levels.

BERRY CITRUS SALAD

Yield: 4 servings | Prep time: 15 minutes | Cook time: 0 minutes

Ingredients:

1 cup strawberries, hulled and halved	2 oranges, peeled and sectioned	2 teaspoons honey (optional)
1 cup blueberries	1 tablespoon fresh mint, chopped	1 teaspoon lemon zest
1 cup blackberries		1 tablespoon lemon juice

Directions:

1. In a large bowl, combine the strawberries, blueberries, blackberries, and orange sections.

2. In a small bowl, whisk together the lemon zest, lemon juice, and honey (if using) to create a light dressing.

3. Pour the dressing over the fruit and gently toss to combine. Sprinkle with fresh mint before serving.

4. Serve immediately or chill in the refrigerator for an hour to allow the flavors to meld.

Nutritional Information. Per serving: 90 calories, 2g protein, 22g carbohydrates, 0.5g fat, 6g fiber, 0mg cholesterol, 0mg sodium, 300mg potassium.

This Diabetic-Friendly Berry Citrus Salad combines a vibrant mix of berries and citrus fruits, offering a refreshing and nutritious option that's low in calories but high in fiber and antioxidants. The hint of mint and lemon adds a fresh, zesty flavor, making it an ideal dessert or snack for those managing diabetes. The optional honey can be adjusted or omitted to suit individual dietary needs, ensuring blood sugar levels remain stable.

5. GRAINS, LEGUMES, BEANS

CHICKPEA AND QUINOA PILAF

Yield: 4 servings | Prep time: 10 minutes | Cook time: 20 minutes

Ingredients:

1 cup quinoa, rinsed	1/2 cup frozen peas	1/2 teaspoon turmeric
2 cups vegetable broth	1 small onion, diced	2 tablespoons olive oil
1 can (15 ounces) chickpeas	2 cloves garlic, minced	Salt and pepper to taste
1 large carrot, diced	1 teaspoon ground cumin	Fresh cilantro for garnish

Directions:

1. Heat the olive oil in a large skillet over medium heat. Add the onion and garlic, and sauté until the onion is translucent, about 5 minutes.

2. Stir in the quinoa, vegetable broth, cumin, and turmeric. Bring to a boil, then reduce heat to low, cover, and simmer for 15 minutes.

3. Add the chickpeas, carrots, and frozen peas to the skillet. Cover and cook for an additional 5 minutes, or until the quinoa is fluffy and the vegetables are tender.

4. Season with salt and pepper to taste. Garnish with fresh cilantro before serving.

Nutritional Information. Per serving: Approximately 320 calories, 12g protein, 54g carbohydrates, 8g fat, 10g fiber, 0mg cholesterol, 300mg sodium, 400mg potassium.

This Chickpea and Quinoa Pilaf is a hearty, nutritious meal perfect for individuals managing diabetes. The combination of quinoa and chickpeas provides a high-fiber, high-protein dish that can help stabilize blood sugar levels. The addition of turmeric and cumin not only brings a burst of flavor but also offers anti-inflammatory benefits. This dish is complete with vegetables for added vitamins and minerals, making it a balanced, diabetes-friendly option that doesn't compromise on taste or nutrition.

QUINOA AND BLACK BEAN SALAD

Yield: 4 servings | Prep time: 15 minutes | Cook time: 20 minutes

Ingredients:

1 cup uncooked quinoa	1 medium red bell pepper, diced	Juice of 1 lime
2 cups water	1/4 cup fresh cilantro, chopped	2 tablespoons olive oil
1 can (15 ounces) black beans, rinsed and drained	2 green onions, thinly sliced	1/2 teaspoon ground cumin
		Salt and pepper to taste

Directions:

1. Rinse the quinoa under cold running water. In a medium saucepan, bring 2 cups of water to a boil. Add the quinoa, reduce heat to low, cover, and simmer for about 15 to 20 minutes, or until the water is absorbed and the quinoa is tender. Remove from heat and let it cool.

2. In a large bowl, combine the cooled quinoa, black beans, red bell pepper, cilantro, and green onions.

3. In a small bowl, whisk together the lime juice, olive oil, ground cumin, salt, and pepper. Pour the dressing over the quinoa mixture and toss to combine.

4. Chill the salad in the refrigerator for at least 1 hour before serving to allow the flavors to meld.

Nutritional Information. Per serving: 320 calories, 12g protein, 45g carbohydrates, 10g fat, 10g fiber, 0mg cholesterol, 200mg sodium, 600mg potassium.

This Quinoa and Black Bean Salad is an excellent diabetic-friendly dish, rich in plant-based protein and fiber, which are crucial for blood sugar control and heart health. The combination of quinoa and black beans provides a complete protein source, while the fiber content helps to slow down the absorption of sugars into the bloodstream. Additionally, the salad is loaded with vitamins and minerals from fresh vegetables and dressed with heart-healthy olive oil and lime juice, making it a nutritious and flavorful choice for anyone managing diabetes.

LENTIL AND BROWN RICE STUFFED BELL PEPPERS

Yield: 4 servings | Prep time: 20 minutes | Cook time: 1 hour

Ingredients:

4 large bell peppers, tops cut away and seeds removed	1 small onion, diced	1/2 teaspoon paprika
1/2 cup brown rice	2 cloves garlic, minced	Salt and pepper to taste
1 cup green lentils	1 can (14.5 ounces) diced tomatoes, drained	1 tablespoon olive oil
2 cups vegetable broth	1 teaspoon ground cumin	1/4 cup shredded low-fat cheese (optional)

Directions:

1. Preheat oven to 350°F (175°C). In a saucepan, bring the vegetable broth to a boil. Add brown rice and lentils, reduce heat to low, cover, and simmer for 45 minutes, or until both are tender and the liquid is absorbed.

2. While the rice and lentils are cooking, heat olive oil in a skillet over medium heat. Add the onion and garlic, sautéing until softened, about 5 minutes. Stir in the diced tomatoes, cumin, paprika, salt, and pepper. Cook for another 5 minutes, then remove from heat.

3. Combine the cooked rice and lentils with the tomato mixture. Adjust seasoning if necessary.

4. Stuff the bell peppers with the lentil and rice mixture, place in a baking dish, and cover with foil. Bake for 30 minutes. Uncover, top with cheese if using, and bake for an additional 10 minutes, or until the cheese is melted and the peppers are tender.

Nutritional Information. Per serving: 350 calories, 18g protein, 60g carbohydrates, 4g fat, 15g fiber, 0mg cholesterol, 300mg sodium, 800mg potassium.

This Lentil and Brown Rice Stuffed Bell Peppers recipe offers a balanced combination of complex carbohydrates, protein, and fiber, making it ideal for individuals managing diabetes. The high fiber content from lentils and brown rice helps in slow sugar absorption, thus maintaining steady blood sugar levels. Moreover, this dish is rich in vitamins and minerals from vegetables and provides a wholesome, satisfying meal with low fat and cholesterol content, catering well to a diabetic diet.

THREE BEAN CHILI WITH QUINOA

Yield: 6 servings | Prep time: 15 minutes | Cook time: 45 minutes

Ingredients:

1 cup quinoa, rinsed	1 can (15 ounces) kidney beans, rinsed and drained	1 tablespoon cumin
2 cups water		1 teaspoon smoked paprika
1 tablespoon olive oil	1 can (15 ounces) pinto beans, rinsed and drained	Salt and pepper to taste
1 large onion, diced		4 cups vegetable broth
3 cloves garlic, minced	1 can (28 ounces) diced tomatoes	Optional toppings: diced avocado, chopped cilantro, low-fat sour cream
1 can (15 ounces) black beans, rinsed and drained	2 tablespoons chili powder	

Directions:

1. In a medium saucepan, combine the quinoa and water. Bring to a boil, then reduce heat to low, cover, and simmer for about 15 minutes, or until the water is absorbed. Remove from heat and set aside.

2. While the quinoa is cooking, heat the olive oil in a large pot over medium heat. Add the onion and garlic, and sauté until soft, about 5 minutes.

3. To the pot, add all three types of beans, diced tomatoes, chili powder, cumin, smoked paprika, salt, pepper, and vegetable broth. Bring the mixture to a simmer, then reduce the heat to low and cook, uncovered, for about 30 minutes, stirring occasionally.

4. Stir in the cooked quinoa and continue to cook for another 10 minutes, allowing the chili to thicken. Adjust seasoning as needed.

5. Serve hot, garnished with optional toppings if desired.

Nutritional Information. Per serving: Approximately 330 calories, 18g protein, 55g carbohydrates, 5g fat, 15g fiber, 0mg cholesterol, 700mg sodium, 900mg potassium.

This Three Bean Chili with Quinoa is a hearty, nutritious meal perfect for diabetics. It's packed with plant-based protein and fiber from the beans and quinoa, which are excellent for blood sugar control. The high fiber content helps slow down the digestion of carbohydrates, preventing spikes in blood sugar levels. Additionally, this chili is low in fat and calories, making it an ideal choice for a healthy, balanced diet. The combination of spices adds a rich flavor without adding unnecessary sodium, making it a delicious and diabetic-friendly option.

CHICKPEA AND SPINACH CURRY

Yield: 4 servings | Prep time: 15 minutes | Cook time: 25 minutes

Ingredients:

2 tablespoons olive oil	1 teaspoon ground cumin	1 can (14.5 ounces) diced tomatoes
1 large onion, diced	1/2 teaspoon turmeric	1 cup light coconut milk
2 cloves garlic, minced	1 can (15 ounces) chickpeas, rinsed and drained	Salt and pepper to taste
1 tablespoon grated ginger	4 cups fresh spinach	Cooked brown rice, for serving
1 tablespoon curry powder		

Directions:

1. Heat the olive oil in a large skillet over medium heat. Add the onion, garlic, and ginger, and sauté until the onion is translucent, about 5 minutes.

2. Stir in the curry powder, cumin, and turmeric, cooking for another minute until fragrant.

3. Add the chickpeas and diced tomatoes (with their juice), bringing the mixture to a simmer. Cook for 10 minutes, allowing the flavors to meld.

4. Stir in the spinach and coconut milk, cooking just until the spinach is wilted and the curry is heated through, about 5 minutes. Season with salt and pepper to taste.

5. Serve the curry over cooked brown rice.

Nutritional Information. Per serving: Approximately 275 calories, 9g protein, 35g carbohydrates, 12g fat, 9g fiber, 0mg cholesterol, 400mg sodium, 700mg potassium.

This Chickpea and Spinach Curry is a flavorful, nutritious option for diabetics, focusing on high-fiber chickpeas and leafy greens. The combination of spices not only adds depth of flavor but also offers anti-inflammatory benefits. The high fiber content helps in managing blood sugar levels by slowing down glucose absorption. This dish is also a good source of plant-based protein and essential nutrients, making it a balanced and satisfying meal for those managing diabetes.

BLACK BEAN AND CORN SALSA WITH WHOLE GRAIN TORTILLA CHIPS

Yield: 4 servings | Prep time: 15 minutes | Cook time: 10 minutes (for the tortilla chips)

Ingredients:

For the Whole Grain Tortilla Chips:	1/2 teaspoon garlic powder	1 medium tomato, diced
	For the Salsa:	1/4 cup onion, finely chopped
4 whole grain tortillas	1 can (15 ounces) black beans, rinsed and drained	1/4 cup cilantro, chopped
1 tablespoon olive oil		Juice of 1 lime
1/2 teaspoon chili powder	1 cup frozen corn, thawed	Salt and pepper to taste

Directions:

1. In a large bowl, combine black beans, corn, tomato, red onion, cilantro, and lime juice. Season with salt and pepper to taste. Mix well and set aside to let the flavors meld.

2. Preheat oven to 375°F (190°C). Brush both sides of the tortillas with olive oil and sprinkle with chili powder and garlic powder. Cut the tortillas into wedges and spread them out in a single layer on a baking sheet.

3. Bake for 8-10 minutes or until crispy and golden brown. Allow the chips to cool before serving them with the salsa.

Nutritional Information. Per serving: Approximately 225 calories, 8g protein, 38g carbohydrates, 5g fat, 8g fiber, 0mg cholesterol, 300mg sodium, 400mg potassium.

This Black Bean and Corn Salsa with Whole Grain Tortilla Chips recipe offers a delicious and nutritious snack option for diabetics. The salsa is rich in fiber and protein from the black beans and provides a good mix of vitamins and minerals from the vegetables. The whole grain tortilla chips are a healthier alternative to store-bought chips, being baked and made from whole grains, which are beneficial for maintaining stable blood sugar levels. This dish combines flavor and health, making it a great choice for anyone looking to enjoy a diabetic-friendly snack.

EDAMAME AND BARLEY SALAD

Yield: 4 servings | Prep time: 15 minutes | Cook time: 30 minutes

Ingredients:

1 cup pearl barley	1 red bell pepper, diced	1/4 cup chopped fresh parsley
3 cups water	1/2 cup diced cucumber	Juice of 1 lemon
1 cup shelled edamame, thawed if frozen	1/4 cup chopped red onion	Salt and pepper to taste
	2 tablespoons olive oil	

Directions:

1. Rinse the barley under cold water. In a medium saucepan, bring the water to a boil. Add the barley, reduce heat to low, cover, and simmer for about 30 minutes, or until the barley is tender and the water is absorbed. Let the barley cool to room temperature.

2. In a large bowl, combine the cooled barley, edamame, red bell pepper, cucumber, red onion, and parsley.

3. In a small bowl, whisk together the olive oil, lemon juice, salt, and pepper. Pour the dressing over the barley salad and toss to combine thoroughly.

4. Chill the salad in the refrigerator for at least 1 hour before serving to allow the flavors to meld together.

Nutritional Information. Per serving: Approximately 300 calories, 10g protein, 45g carbohydrates, 8g fat, 10g fiber, 0mg cholesterol, 15mg sodium, 350mg potassium.

This Edamame and Barley Salad is a vibrant, nutritious dish that's especially suitable for diabetics. The combination of fiber-rich barley and protein-packed edamame makes it an excellent choice for blood sugar management. The fiber helps to slow digestion and prevent spikes in blood glucose levels, while the protein is essential for muscle repair and maintenance. The added vegetables provide vitamins and antioxidants, making this salad not just a delight for the palate but also a boost for overall health.

LENTIL AND VEGETABLE SOUP WITH BARLEY

Yield: 6 servings | Prep time: 15 minutes | Cook time: 1 hour

Ingredients:

1 cup dried green lentils, rinsed	2 stalks celery, diced	1 teaspoon dried thyme
1/2 cup pearl barley, rinsed	2 cloves garlic, minced	1 bay leaf
2 tablespoons olive oil	1 can (14.5 ounces) diced tomatoes	Salt and pepper to taste
1 large onion, diced		2 cups chopped kale or spinach
2 carrots, peeled and diced	6 cups vegetable broth	Juice of 1 lemon

Directions:

1. In a large pot, heat the olive oil over medium heat. Add the onion, carrots, celery, and garlic, sautéing until the vegetables are softened, about 5 minutes.

2. Add the lentils, barley, diced tomatoes (with their juice), vegetable broth, thyme, bay leaf, salt, and pepper. Bring the mixture to a boil, then reduce the heat to low and simmer, covered, for about 50 minutes or until the lentils and barley are tender.

3. Stir in the chopped kale or spinach and continue to simmer until the greens have wilted about 5 minutes. Remove the bay leaf, and stir in the lemon juice. Adjust seasoning as needed.

4. Serve hot, offering a comforting and nutritious meal.

Nutritional Information. Per serving: Approximately 220 calories, 12g protein, 40g carbohydrates, 3g fat, 15g fiber, 0mg cholesterol, 300mg sodium, 600mg potassium.

This Lentil and Vegetable Soup with Barley is a hearty, comforting meal perfect for diabetics, providing a good balance of complex carbohydrates, protein, and fiber. The fiber from lentils, barley, and vegetables helps to slow digestion and prevent spikes in blood glucose levels, making it an excellent choice for blood sugar management. The addition of kale or spinach adds a boost of vitamins and minerals, enhancing the nutritional profile of the soup. This soup is not only nutritious but also flavorful and satisfying, making it a great addition to a diabetic-friendly diet.

BEAN AND FARRO BUDDHA BOWL

Yield: 4 servings | Prep time: 15 minutes | Cook time: 30 minutes

Ingredients:

1 cup farro, rinsed	1 avocado, sliced	1/4 cup tahini
2 cups water	2 cups roasted vegetables	Juice of 1 lemon
1 can (15 ounces) black beans, rinsed and drained	(such as bell peppers, zucchini, and cherry tomatoes)	Salt and pepper to taste
2 cups fresh spinach		Optional: pumpkin seeds or sunflower seeds for garnish

Directions:

1. In a medium saucepan, combine the farro and water. Bring to a boil, then reduce heat to low, cover, and simmer for about 30 minutes, or until the farro is tender and the water is absorbed.

2. While the farro is cooking, prepare the roasted vegetables, if not already done, and rinse and drain the black beans.

3. To assemble the Buddha bowls, divide the cooked farro among four bowls. Top each with an equal portion of black beans, roasted vegetables, and fresh spinach.

4. Drizzle each bowl with tahini, squeeze lemon juice over the top, and season with salt and pepper to taste. Garnish with avocado slices and optional pumpkin seeds or sunflower seeds.

Nutritional Information. Per serving: 400 calories, 15g protein, 60g carbohydrates, 12g fat, 15g fiber, 0mg cholesterol, 300mg sodium, 800mg potassium.

The Bean and Farro Buddha Bowl is a nutrient-dense meal that's perfect for individuals with diabetes. It offers a healthy balance of complex carbohydrates from farro and beans, essential for steady blood sugar levels, along with high fiber to aid in digestion and satiety. The addition of fresh and roasted vegetables contributes vitamins, minerals, and antioxidants, while the avocado provides healthy fats. This meal is a well-rounded option that supports blood sugar management and overall health.

BLACK BEAN AND BROWN RICE BURRITO BOWL

Yield: 4 servings | Prep time: 10 minutes | Cook time: 45 minutes

Ingredients:

1 cup brown rice	1 cup corn kernels,	2 tablespoons cilantro, chopped
2 cups water	1 cup cherry tomatoes, halved	Salt and pepper to taste
1 can (15 ounces) black beans, rinsed and drained	1/4 cup red onion, finely chopped	Optional: 1/4 teaspoon cumin for seasoning
1 large avocado, diced	1 lime, juiced	

Directions:

1. Rinse the brown rice under cold water. In a medium saucepan, bring 2 cups of water to a boil. Add the rice, reduce heat to low, cover, and simmer for about 45 minutes, or until the rice is tender and the water is absorbed.

2. In a large bowl, combine the cooked brown rice, black beans, corn, avocado, cherry tomatoes, red onion, lime juice, cilantro, and optional cumin. Season with salt and pepper to taste, and gently toss to combine all the ingredients.

3. Divide the mixture among four bowls, serving immediately. For added flavor, you can also include a dollop of Greek yogurt or a sprinkle of shredded cheese on top, if desired.

Nutritional Information. Per serving: Approximately 350 calories, 12g protein, 60g carbohydrates, 8g fat, 10g fiber, 0mg cholesterol, 200mg sodium, 700mg potassium.

This Black Bean and Brown Rice Burrito Bowl is an excellent meal choice for diabetics, offering a well-balanced mix of complex carbohydrates, fiber, and protein. The brown rice and black beans provide a stable energy source and help maintain healthy blood sugar levels, while the fiber content aids in digestion and satiety. The addition of fresh vegetables and lime juice not only enhances the flavor but also contributes essential vitamins, minerals, and antioxidants, making this dish both nutritious and delicious.

6. BEEF, PORK AND LAMB

GRILLED FLANK STEAK WITH CHIMICHURRI

Yield: 4 servings | Prep time: 15 minutes (plus marinating time) | Cook time: 10 minutes

Ingredients:

1.5 lbs flank steak	1 cup fresh parsley, finely chopped	3 garlic cloves, minced
Salt and pepper to taste		1 teaspoon red pepper flakes
1/4 cup olive oil	3 tablespoons red wine vinegar	1/2 teaspoon salt

Directions:

1. Season the flank steak on both sides with salt and pepper. Let it sit at room temperature for about 30 minutes before grilling.

2. Preheat the grill to high. Grill the steak for 5 minutes on each side for medium-rare, or until it reaches your desired level of doneness.

3. While the steak is grilling, prepare the chimichurri by combining the parsley, olive oil, red wine vinegar, minced garlic, red pepper flakes, and salt in a bowl. Mix well.

4. Let the steak rest for 5 minutes after grilling. Slice it thinly against the grain and serve with the chimichurri sauce spooned over the top.

Nutritional Information. Per serving: 310 calories, 32g protein, 2g carbohydrates, 20g fat, 0g fiber, 90mg cholesterol, 340mg sodium, 500mg potassium.

This Grilled Flank Steak with Chimichurri recipe is a hearty, flavorful option perfect for diabetics looking for a high-protein, low-carbohydrate meal. The chimichurri sauce adds a fresh, herby, and slightly spicy flavor to the beef without adding excess sugar or carbs, making it an ideal choice for managing blood sugar levels. This dish combines simplicity and taste, offering a satisfying meal that supports a healthy, balanced diet.

BEEF BRISKET

Yield: 4 servings | Prep time: 20 minutes | Cook time: 3 hours

Ingredients:

2 lbs beef brisket	2 cloves garlic, minced	1 teaspoon dried thyme
2 tablespoons olive oil	1 cup low-sodium beef broth	Salt and pepper to taste
1 large onion, sliced	1 tablespoon apple cider vinegar	2 bay leaves

Directions:

1. Preheat the oven to 300°F (150°C). Season the brisket on all sides with salt and pepper.

2. Heat olive oil in a large oven-proof pot over medium-high heat. Add the brisket and sear on both sides until browned, about 3-4 minutes per side. Remove the brisket and set aside.

3. In the same pot, add the onion and garlic, sautéing until softened, about 5 minutes. Return the brisket to the pot. Add the beef broth, apple cider vinegar, thyme, and bay leaves. Bring to a simmer.

4. Cover the pot and transfer it to the preheated oven. Bake for about 3 hours, or until the brisket is tender.

5. Let the brisket rest for 10 minutes before slicing. Serve with the onions and a bit of the cooking liquid.

Nutritional Information. Per serving: 300 calories, 35g protein, 5g carbohydrates, 15g fat, 1g fiber, 85mg cholesterol, 200mg sodium, 600mg potassium.

This Beef Brisket recipe is designed to be diabetic-friendly, focusing on low carbohydrates and high protein, making it suitable for managing blood sugar levels. The use of low-sodium beef broth and minimal added sugars helps to keep the overall sodium and sugar content low, while the olive oil provides healthy fats. This dish combines delicious flavors and tender beef in a way that's both satisfying and aligned with the dietary needs of individuals managing diabetes.

BEEF BOURGUIGNON

Yield: 4 servings | Prep time: 20 minutes | Cook time: 2 hours 30 minutes

Ingredients:

2 lbs beef chuck, cut into 2-inch cubes	2 cups red wine	8 ounces mushrooms, quartered
2 tablespoons olive oil	2 carrots, sliced	Salt and pepper to taste
1/4 cup low-sodium beef broth	2 cloves garlic, minced	2 tablespoons chopped fresh parsley for garnish
1 onion, chopped	1 teaspoon dried thyme	
	1 bay leaf	

Directions:

1. Preheat the oven to 325°F (165°C). Season the beef with salt and pepper. Heat 1 tablespoon of olive oil in a large Dutch oven over medium-high heat. Add the beef in batches and sear until browned on all sides. Transfer to a plate.

2. In the same pot, add the remaining olive oil, onion, carrots, and garlic. Sauté until the vegetables are softened, about 5 minutes.

3. Return the beef to the pot. Add the beef broth, red wine, thyme, and bay leaf. Bring to a simmer, then cover and transfer to the oven. Cook for 2 hours.

4. After 2 hours, add the mushrooms to the pot and cook for an additional 30 minutes, or until the beef is tender.

5. Adjust seasoning with salt and pepper, and garnish with fresh parsley before serving.

Nutritional Information. Per serving: 450 calories, 40g protein, 15g carbohydrates, 20g fat, 3g fiber, 95mg cholesterol, 250mg sodium, 800mg potassium.

This Beef Bourguignon recipe is adapted for a diabetic diet, offering rich flavors without excess carbohydrates. The use of dry red wine with lower sugar content and low-sodium beef broth helps manage sugar and sodium intake. The dish is high in protein and moderate in fat, making it a hearty and satisfying meal that aligns with the nutritional needs of individuals managing diabetes.

GRILLED SIRLOIN WITH MUSTARD RUB

Yield: 4 servings | Prep time: 10 minutes | Cook time: 15 minutes

Ingredients:

4 sirloin steaks (6 ounces each)	1 tablespoon olive oil	2 teaspoons dried thyme
2 tablespoons Dijon mustard	2 teaspoons garlic powder	Salt and pepper to taste

Directions:

1. Preheat the grill to medium-high heat. In a small bowl, combine Dijon mustard, olive oil, garlic powder, dried thyme, salt, and pepper to create a paste.
2. Rub the paste evenly over both sides of each sirloin steak.
3. Place the steaks on the grill and cook for about 7-8 minutes per side for medium-rare, or until they reach your desired level of doneness.
4. Let the steaks rest for 5 minutes after grilling to allow the juices to redistribute.
5. Serve the steaks hot, optionally garnished with fresh thyme or parsley.

Nutritional Information. Per serving: 290 calories, 35g protein, 1g carbohydrates, 16g fat, 0g fiber, 95mg cholesterol, 320mg sodium, 550mg potassium.

This Grilled Sirloin with Mustard Rub recipe provides a simple yet flavorful option for diabetics, focusing on high-quality protein and healthy fats. The mustard rub infuses the beef with a tangy and aromatic flavor, enhancing the natural taste of the sirloin without adding unnecessary sugars or carbs. This meal is both satisfying and nutritious, making it an excellent choice for those managing diabetes and looking for delicious, heart-healthy grilling options.

BEEF STROGANOFF

Yield: 4 servings | Prep time: 15 minutes | Cook time: 25 minutes

Ingredients:

1 lb lean beef sirloin, thinly sliced	8 ounces mushrooms, sliced	Salt and pepper to taste
2 tablespoons olive oil	1 cup low-sodium beef broth	2 tablespoons fresh parsley, chopped (for garnish)
1 medium onion, finely chopped	1 teaspoon Dijon mustard	Optional: Serve with whole-grain noodles or cauliflower rice
2 cloves garlic, minced	1/2 cup sour cream (use a low-fat variety for a healthier option)	

Directions:

1. Heat 1 tablespoon of olive oil in a large skillet over medium-high heat. Add the beef slices and cook until browned. Remove the beef from the skillet and set aside.

2. In the same skillet, add the remaining olive oil, onion, garlic, and mushrooms. Sauté until the vegetables are soft, about 5-7 minutes.

3. Return the beef to the skillet and add the beef broth and Dijon mustard. Bring to a simmer and cook for 5 minutes.

4. Reduce the heat to low and stir in the sour cream. Cook until the sauce is heated through but not boiling. Season with salt and pepper to taste.

5. Garnish with fresh parsley before serving. Serve over whole-grain noodles or cauliflower rice for a complete meal.

Nutritional Information. Per serving: Approximately 300 calories, 25g protein, 10g carbohydrates, 18g fat, 2g fiber, 75mg cholesterol, 200mg sodium, 500mg potassium.

This Beef Stroganoff recipe is tailored for individuals managing diabetes, focusing on lean protein and low-fat dairy options to reduce overall calorie and fat intake. By serving it with whole-grain noodles or cauliflower rice, you can enjoy a classic comfort dish while maintaining a balanced diet that supports healthy blood sugar levels. The recipe offers a good mix of protein, healthy fats, and fiber, making it a satisfying and nutritious option for a diabetic-friendly meal.

BEEF WELLINGTON

Yield: 4 servings | Prep time: 30 minutes | Cook time: 40 minutes

Ingredients:

1 lb beef tenderloin 2 tablespoons olive oil 1/2 teaspoon salt 1/4 teaspoon black pepper	2 cups mushrooms, finely chopped 1 medium onion, finely chopped 2 cloves garlic, minced	4 slices of whole-grain or low-carb tortillas (as a substitute for puff pastry) 1 egg, beaten (for egg wash)

Directions:

1. Preheat the oven to 400°F (200°C). Season the beef with salt and pepper. Heat 1 tablespoon of olive oil in a skillet over high heat. Sear the beef on all sides until browned, about 2-3 minutes per side. Remove from the skillet and let it cool.

2. In the same skillet, add the remaining olive oil, mushrooms, onion, and garlic. Sauté over medium heat until all the moisture has evaporated and the mixture is well browned, about 10 minutes. Let it cool.

3. Lay out the tortillas and spread the mushroom mixture in the center of each. Place the beef on top of the mushroom mixture. Roll up tightly, trimming any excess tortilla, and seal the edges with a bit of beaten egg.

4. Place the wrapped beef seam-side down on a baking sheet lined with parchment paper. Brush with beaten egg. Bake for 20-25 minutes or until the tortillas are golden and crisp.

5. Let the beef rest for 10 minutes before slicing and serving.

Nutritional Information. Per serving: 50 calories, 28g protein, 18g carbohydrates, 18g fat, 3g fiber, 95mg cholesterol, 320mg sodium, 500mg potassium.

This Beef Wellington adaptation offers a more diabetic-friendly approach by using whole-grain or low-carb tortillas instead of traditional puff pastry, significantly reducing the dish's overall carbohydrate content. The focus is on lean protein from the beef tenderloin and nutrients from the mushrooms and onions, making it suitable for a diabetic diet while still providing a sense of indulgence.

BEEF POT ROAST

Yield: 6 servings | Prep time: 20 minutes | Cook time: 4 hours

Ingredients:

3 lbs beef chuck roast	4 cups low-sodium beef broth	2 stalks celery, cut into 2-inch pieces
2 tablespoons olive oil	1 onion, quartered	1 teaspoon dried thyme
1/2 teaspoon salt	2 carrots, cut into 2-inch pieces	1 bay leaf
1/4 teaspoon black pepper	2 cloves garlic, minced	

Directions:

1. Season the beef chuck roast with salt and pepper. Heat olive oil in a large pot or Dutch oven over medium-high heat. Add the roast and sear on all sides until browned, about 3-4 minutes per side.

2. Add the low-sodium beef broth to the pot along with the onion, carrots, celery, garlic, thyme, and bay leaf. Bring to a simmer.

3. Once simmering, cover the pot and reduce the heat to low. Let it cook for about 4 hours, or until the beef is tender and falls apart easily.

4. Remove the bay leaf and shred the beef with two forks. Serve the beef with the vegetables and a bit of the cooking liquid.

Nutritional Information. Per serving: 400 calories, 35g protein, 10g carbohydrates, 25g fat, 2g fiber, 120mg cholesterol, 200mg sodium, 600mg potassium.

This Beef Pot Roast recipe is tailored for individuals managing diabetes, focusing on high-quality protein and low-carbohydrate vegetables. The use of low-sodium beef broth and the addition of whole vegetables ensure that the dish is full of flavor without adding unnecessary sodium or sugars, making it a hearty and healthy option for a diabetic-friendly diet.

BEEF SHEPHERD'S PIE

Yield: 4 servings | Prep time: 30 minutes | Cook time: 30 minutes

Ingredients:

1 lb lean ground beef	1 tablespoon tomato paste	2 cups mashed cauliflower (as a substitute for mashed potatoes)
2 tablespoons olive oil	1 teaspoon Worcestershire sauce	
1 onion, diced		
2 carrots, diced	1/2 cup low-sodium beef broth	1/4 cup grated Parmesan cheese (optional for topping)
2 cloves garlic, minced		
1 cup frozen peas	Salt and pepper to taste	

Directions:

1. Preheat the oven to 375°F (190°C). Heat the olive oil in a large skillet over medium heat. Add the onion, carrots, and garlic, cooking until softened, about 5 minutes.

2. Increase the heat to medium-high, add the ground beef to the skillet, and cook until browned, breaking it up with a spoon as it cooks. Drain any excess fat.

3. Stir in the frozen peas, tomato paste, Worcestershire sauce, and beef broth. Simmer for about 10 minutes, or until the liquid has slightly reduced. Season with salt and pepper.

4. Spread the beef mixture in an even layer in a baking dish. Top with mashed cauliflower, smoothing it out with a spoon. Sprinkle with Parmesan cheese if using.

5. Bake for 20-25 minutes, or until the top is slightly golden and the edges are bubbling. Let it cool for a few minutes before serving.

Nutritional Information. Per serving: 350 calories, 26g protein, 18g carbohydrates, 18g fat, 5g fiber, 70mg cholesterol, 300mg sodium, 700mg potassium.

This Beef Shepherd's Pie recipe offers a diabetic-friendly twist on the traditional dish by substituting mashed potatoes with mashed cauliflower, significantly reducing the carbohydrate content while still delivering a comforting and satisfying meal. The use of lean ground beef and low-sodium beef broth helps to keep the fat and sodium levels in check, making it a healthier option for individuals managing diabetes.

BEEF CHILI

Yield: 6 servings | Prep time: 15 minutes | Cook time: 1 hour

Ingredients:

2 lbs lean ground beef	2 cans (15 ounces each) low-sodium diced tomatoes	Salt and pepper to taste
1 tablespoon olive oil	1 can (15 ounces) low-sodium kidney beans	Water, as needed for desired consistency
1 large onion, diced	1 teaspoon ground cumin	Optional garnishes: chopped green onions, shredded low-fat cheese
2 cloves garlic, minced	1/2 teaspoon paprika	
1 bell pepper, diced		
2 tablespoons chili powder		

Directions:

1. Heat the olive oil in a large pot over medium heat. Add the onion, garlic, and bell pepper. Cook until softened, about 5 minutes.

2. Increase the heat to medium-high and add the lean ground beef to the pot. Cook, breaking it apart with a spoon, until browned. Drain any excess fat.

3. Add the diced tomatoes (with their juice), kidney beans, chili powder, cumin, paprika, salt, and pepper to the pot. Stir well to combine.

4. Bring the mixture to a simmer, then reduce the heat to low. Cover and cook for about 45 minutes to 1 hour, stirring occasionally. Add water as needed to adjust the consistency according to preference.

5. Serve hot, garnished with green onions and shredded cheese if desired.

Nutritional Information. Per serving: 300 calories, 35g protein, 20g carbohydrates, 10g fat, 6g fiber, 70mg cholesterol, 300mg sodium, 800mg potassium.

This Beef Chili recipe is designed to be diabetic-friendly, focusing on high protein and fiber while keeping the fat, sodium, and carbohydrate levels in moderation. The use of lean ground beef and low-sodium canned products helps to make this dish both hearty and healthy, perfect for managing blood sugar levels. The rich spices contribute to a flavorful experience without the need for added sugars or high-sodium seasonings, making it a nutritious and satisfying meal for anyone, especially those managing diabetes.

BEEF LASAGNA

Yield: 6 servings | Prep time: 30 minutes | Cook time: 1 hour

Ingredients:

1 lb lean ground beef 1 tablespoon olive oil 1 large onion, chopped 2 cloves garlic, minced 1 can (15 ounces) low-sodium tomato sauce 1/2 cup water	1 can (6 ounces) low-sodium tomato paste 1 teaspoon dried oregano 1 teaspoon dried basil Salt and pepper to taste 9 whole-grain lasagna noodles 1 large egg	1.5 cups ricotta cheese (low-fat) 2 cups fresh spinach, chopped 2 cups shredded mozzarella cheese (low-fat) 1/4 cup grated Parmesan cheese (low-fat)

Directions:

1. Preheat the oven to 375°F (190°C). In a large skillet, heat the olive oil over medium heat. Add the onion and garlic, sautéing until softened. Add the ground beef and cook until browned. Drain any excess fat.

2. Stir in the tomato sauce, tomato paste, water, oregano, basil, salt, and pepper. Simmer for about 15 minutes to blend the flavors. Set aside.

3. Cook the lasagna noodles according to package instructions; drain and set aside.

4. In a bowl, mix the ricotta cheese, egg, and spinach. Season with a pinch of salt and pepper.

5. To assemble, spread a thin layer of the meat sauce in the bottom of a 9x13-inch baking dish. Layer with noodles, half of the ricotta mixture, and a portion of the mozzarella, and repeat, ending with a layer of noodles topped with meat sauce. Sprinkle the remaining mozzarella and Parmesan cheese on top.

6. Cover with foil and bake for 25 minutes. Remove the foil and bake for an additional 10 minutes or until the cheese is bubbly and slightly browned. Let it cool for 10 minutes before serving.

Nutritional Information. Per serving: 410 calories, 32g protein, 38g carbohydrates, 15g fat, 6g fiber, 85mg cholesterol, 420mg sodium, 700mg potassium.

This Beef Lasagna recipe has been modified to be more diabetic-friendly by incorporating lean ground beef, whole-grain noodles, and low-fat cheeses. The use of low-sodium tomato products helps to reduce the overall sodium content. The addition of fresh spinach boosts the nutritional profile, providing fiber, vitamins, and minerals. This dish is a comforting, hearty meal that can be enjoyed by those managing diabetes without compromising on traditional flavors.

BEEF TACOS

Yield: 4 servings | Prep time: 15 minutes | Cook time: 10 minutes

Ingredients:

1 lb lean ground beef	1 tablespoon homemade or low-sodium taco seasoning	1 tomato, diced
1 tablespoon olive oil		1/2 cup shredded low-fat cheese
1/2 cup onion, diced	8 small whole-grain or low-carb tortillas	1/4 cup plain Greek yogurt (as a sour cream substitute)
2 cloves garlic, minced		
1/2 cup low-sodium beef broth	1 cup lettuce, shredded	Optional: salsa, lime wedges

Directions:

1. Heat olive oil in a large skillet over medium heat. Add onion and garlic, cooking until softened, about 3 minutes.

2. Increase heat to medium-high and add the ground beef to the skillet. Cook, breaking it apart with a spoon, until browned and no longer pink. Drain any excess fat.

3. Stir in the taco seasoning and beef broth. Simmer until the liquid has reduced and the mixture is thickened about 5 minutes.

4. Warm the tortillas according to package instructions. Divide the beef mixture among the tortillas.

5. Top each taco with lettuce, tomato, cheese, and a dollop of Greek yogurt. Serve with optional salsa and lime wedges on the side.

Nutritional Information. Per serving: 350 calories, 26g protein, 28g carbohydrates, 16g fat, 6g fiber, 70mg cholesterol, 320mg sodium, 500mg potassium.

These Beef Tacos are tailored for a diabetic diet, emphasizing lean protein, fiber-rich whole grains, and low-fat dairy options. The use of homemade or low-sodium taco seasoning reduces the sodium content often found in store-bought mixes, making it a healthier choice for maintaining balanced blood sugar levels. The addition of fresh vegetables and the substitution of Greek yogurt for sour cream increase the nutritional value while keeping the dish flavorful and satisfying.

BEEF SHORT RIBS

Yield: 4 servings | Prep time: 20 minutes | Cook time: 2 hours 30 minutes

Ingredients:

2 lbs beef short ribs, trimmed of excess fat	2 stalks celery, chopped	1 cup dry red wine (can be replaced with beef broth for a non-alcoholic version)
2 tablespoons olive oil	2 cloves garlic, minced	
1 large onion, chopped	1 cup low-sodium beef broth	
2 carrots, chopped	1 tablespoon tomato paste	1 bay leaf
	1 teaspoon dried thyme	Salt and pepper to taste

Directions:

1. Preheat the oven to 325°F (165°C). Season the short ribs with salt and pepper. Heat olive oil in a large oven-proof Dutch oven over medium-high heat. Add the short ribs and sear on all sides until browned, about 3-4 minutes per side. Remove the ribs and set aside.

2. In the same Dutch oven, add the onion, carrots, celery, and garlic. Cook over medium heat until the vegetables begin to soften, about 5 minutes.

3. Stir in the tomato paste, thyme, and bay leaf. Add the beef broth and red wine (or additional beef broth). Bring to a simmer.

4. Return the short ribs to the pot. Cover with a lid or tightly with foil and place in the oven. Bake for about 2 to 2.5 hours, or until the meat is tender and falls off the bone.

5. Remove the bay leaf and skim off any excess fat from the surface of the sauce. Serve the ribs with the vegetables and sauce.

Nutritional Information. Per serving: 400 calories, 24g protein, 8g carbohydrates, 25g fat, 2g fiber, 100mg cholesterol, 200mg sodium, 500mg potassium.

This Beef Short Ribs recipe offers a diabetic-friendly option by focusing on lean protein, nutrient-rich vegetables, and low-sodium ingredients. The optional use of red wine adds depth to the dish but can be substituted with beef broth to reduce the sugar content, making it adaptable for those managing diabetes. The slow cooking process ensures the meat is tender and flavorful, creating a hearty and satisfying meal.

PORK TENDERLOIN

Yield: 4 servings | Prep time: 15 minutes | Cook time: 25 minutes

Ingredients:

1 pork tenderloin (about 1 lb) 2 tablespoons olive oil 1 teaspoon garlic powder 1 teaspoon dried thyme	1/2 teaspoon smoked paprika Salt and pepper to taste 1 tablespoon Dijon mustard	1/4 cup low-sodium chicken broth 1 tablespoon apple cider vinegar

Directions:

1. Preheat your oven to 375°F (190°C). In a small bowl, mix the garlic powder, dried thyme, smoked paprika, salt, and pepper. Rub this mixture all over the pork tenderloin.

2. Heat the olive oil in an oven-safe skillet over medium-high heat. Add the pork tenderloin and sear it on all sides until golden brown, about 2-3 minutes per side.

3. In a small bowl, whisk together the low-sodium chicken broth, Dijon mustard, and apple cider vinegar. Pour this mixture over the seared pork in the skillet.

4. Transfer the skillet to the preheated oven and roast the pork for about 15-20 minutes, or until a meat thermometer inserted into the thickest part of the tenderloin reads 145°F (63°C).

5. Let the pork rest for 5 minutes before slicing. Serve with the sauce from the skillet drizzled over the top.

Nutritional Information. Per serving: 220 calories, 24g protein, 2g carbohydrates, 13g fat, 0g fiber, 75mg cholesterol, 200mg sodium, 400mg potassium.

This Pork Tenderloin recipe is designed with diabetic dietary needs in mind, featuring lean protein and low in carbohydrates. The use of spices and low-sodium broth for flavoring reduces the need for added salt, making it a heart-healthy choice. The addition of Dijon mustard and apple cider vinegar introduces a depth of flavor without adding sugar, aligning with a diabetic-friendly diet. This dish provides a satisfying and nutritious option for those looking to maintain balanced blood sugar levels.

PORK STIR-FRY

Yield: 4 servings | Prep time: 15 minutes | Cook time: 10 minutes

Ingredients:

1 lb pork tenderloin, thinly sliced	1 carrot, sliced thinly	1 tablespoon apple cider vinegar
2 tablespoons olive oil	2 green onions, chopped	1 teaspoon sesame oil
2 cups broccoli florets	2 cloves garlic, minced	Optional: 1 teaspoon sugar substitute for balance
1 red bell pepper, sliced	1 tablespoon grated ginger	
	1/4 cup low-sodium soy sauce	Salt and pepper to taste

Directions:

1. Heat 1 tablespoon of olive oil in a large skillet or wok over medium-high heat. Add the pork slices and stir-fry until browned and cooked through, about 3-4 minutes. Remove pork from the skillet and set aside.

2. In the same skillet, add the remaining tablespoon of olive oil. Add the broccoli, bell pepper, carrot, green onions, garlic, and ginger. Stir-fry until the vegetables are just tender, about 3-5 minutes.

3. In a small bowl, whisk together the low-sodium soy sauce, apple cider vinegar, sesame oil, and optional sugar substitute. Pour this sauce over the cooked vegetables in the skillet.

4. Return the cooked pork to the skillet. Toss everything together and cook for an additional 2 minutes, allowing the flavors to meld.

5. Season with salt and pepper to taste. Serve immediately.

Nutritional Information. Per serving: 250 calories, 26g protein, 10g carbohydrates, 12g fat, 3g fiber, 75mg cholesterol, 450mg sodium, 600mg potassium.

This Pork Stir-Fry recipe is tailored for individuals managing diabetes, emphasizing lean protein, high-fiber vegetables, and low-sodium ingredients. The inclusion of a sugar substitute offers a hint of sweetness without impacting blood sugar levels significantly, making it a balanced and flavorful option for a diabetic-friendly meal. The dish is nutrient-dense, providing a good mix of vitamins, minerals, and antioxidants, alongside the protein and fiber needed for blood sugar management.

GRILLED PORK CHOPS

Yield: 4 servings | Prep time: 10 minutes (plus at least 1 hour for marinating) | Cook time: 12 minutes

Ingredients:

4 boneless pork chops, about 1-inch thick	2 cloves garlic, minced	Juice of 1 lemon
2 tablespoons olive oil	1 teaspoon dried thyme	Salt and pepper to taste
	1 teaspoon dried rosemary	

Directions:

1. In a small bowl, whisk together olive oil, garlic, thyme, rosemary, lemon juice, salt, and pepper to create a marinade.

2. Place pork chops in a resealable plastic bag or shallow dish. Pour the marinade over the pork chops, making sure they are well coated. Seal or cover, and marinate in the refrigerator for at least 1 hour, or overnight for best results.

3. Preheat the grill to medium-high heat. Remove the pork chops from the marinade, letting the excess drip off. Grill the pork chops for about 5-6 minutes per side, or until they reach an internal temperature of 145°F (63°C).

4. Let the pork chops rest for 3 minutes after removing them from the grill. This helps the juices redistribute throughout the meat, ensuring it's moist and flavorful.

5. Serve the grilled pork chops with a side of grilled vegetables or a fresh salad for a complete diabetic-friendly meal.

Nutritional Information. Per serving: 220 calories, 25g protein, 1g carbohydrates, 13g fat, 0g fiber, 75mg cholesterol, 200mg sodium, 400mg potassium.

These Grilled Pork Chops are a perfect option for individuals with diabetes, focusing on high-quality protein and healthy fats from olive oil. The use of herbs and lemon juice for marinating adds flavor without contributing extra sugar or carbohydrates, making this dish both delicious and suitable for a diabetic diet. Grilling as a cooking method also reduces the need for added fats, ensuring the meal remains heart-healthy.

PULLED PORK (WITHOUT SUGARY SAUCES)

Yield: 6 servings | Prep time: 15 minutes | Cook time: 8 hours (slow cooker)

Ingredients:

3 lbs pork shoulder 2 tablespoons olive oil 1 tablespoon smoked paprika 1 teaspoon garlic powder 1 teaspoon onion powder	1/2 teaspoon cayenne pepper 1 teaspoon ground cumin Salt and pepper to taste 1/2 cup low-sodium chicken broth	2 tablespoons apple cider vinegar 2 tablespoons Worcestershire sauce (check for sugar content, use a low-sugar version)

Directions:

1. Mix the smoked paprika, garlic powder, onion powder, cayenne pepper, ground cumin, salt, and pepper in a small bowl. Rub this spice mixture all over the pork shoulder.

2. Heat the olive oil in a large skillet over medium-high heat. Sear the pork on all sides until golden brown, about 2-3 minutes per side.

3. Place the seared pork in the slow cooker. Pour the low-sodium chicken broth, apple cider vinegar, and Worcestershire sauce over the pork.

4. Cover and cook on low for 8 hours, or until the pork is tender and shreds easily with a fork.

5. Remove the pork from the slow cooker and shred it using two forks. If desired, you can mix some of the cooking juices back into the pulled pork for additional moisture and flavor.

6. Serve the pulled pork with a side of steamed vegetables or a salad for a complete diabetic-friendly meal.

Nutritional Information. Per serving: 310 calories, 38g protein, 2g carbohydrates, 16g fat, 0g fiber, 105mg cholesterol, 220mg sodium, 600mg potassium.

This Pulled Pork recipe is designed specifically for diabetics, avoiding sugary sauces and focusing on rich, savory flavors from spices and low-sugar liquids. The use of lean pork shoulder and careful seasoning creates a delicious dish that's low in carbohydrates and sugars, making it suitable for managing blood sugar levels. The slow cooking process ensures the pork is tender and flavorful, perfect for a satisfying diabetic-friendly meal.

PORK LOIN ROAST

Yield: 6 servings | Prep time: 20 minutes | Cook time: 1 hour

Ingredients:

2 lbs pork loin roast 2 tablespoons olive oil 1 tablespoon thyme, minced	1 tablespoon rosemary, minced 2 cloves garlic, minced	Salt and pepper to taste 1 cup low-sodium chicken broth

Directions:

1. Preheat your oven to 375°F (190°C). In a small bowl, combine olive oil, rosemary, thyme, garlic, salt, and pepper to create a herb rub.

2. Pat the pork loin dry with paper towels. Rub the entire surface of the pork loin with the herb mixture, making sure it's evenly coated.

3. Place the pork loin in a roasting pan. Pour the low-sodium chicken broth into the bottom of the pan to help keep the pork moist during cooking and to add flavor.

4. Roast in the preheated oven for about 1 hour, or until a meat thermometer inserted into the thickest part of the loin reads 145°F (63°C). Baste the pork occasionally with the pan juices.

5. Let the pork loin rest for at least 10 minutes before slicing. This allows the juices to redistribute throughout the meat, ensuring it's moist and flavorful.

6. Serve slices of the pork loin with a side of steamed vegetables or a salad for a complete diabetic-friendly meal.

Nutritional Information. Per serving: 220 calories, 25g protein, 1g carbohydrates, 13g fat, 0g fiber, 70mg cholesterol, 200mg sodium, 400mg potassium.

This Pork Loin Roast recipe is tailored for a diabetic diet, focusing on lean protein and flavored with low-carbohydrate herbs and spices. The use of low-sodium chicken broth not only adds moisture but also helps to control the sodium content, making it a heart-healthy option. By keeping the dish simple and using fresh ingredients, it offers a nutritious, balanced meal that fits well into a diabetic meal plan.

PORK CARNITAS (USING LEAN CUTS)

Yield: 6 servings | Prep time: 20 minutes | Cook time: 3 hours

Ingredients:

2 lbs lean pork shoulder	1 onion, chopped	1 orange, juice and zest
1 teaspoon salt	3 cloves garlic, minced	1 lime, juice only
1/2 teaspoon black pepper	1 teaspoon ground cumin	2 cups low-sodium
1 tablespoon olive oil	1 teaspoon dried oregano	chicken broth

Directions:

1. Preheat your oven to 300°F (150°C). Season the pork shoulder all over with salt and pepper.
2. Heat olive oil in a large Dutch oven over medium-high heat. Add the pork and sear on all sides until browned, about 3-4 minutes per side.
3. Remove the pork and set aside. In the same pot, add the onion and garlic, cooking until softened, about 5 minutes. Stir in the cumin and oregano.
4. Return the pork to the pot. Add the orange juice and zest, lime juice, and chicken broth. Bring to a simmer, then cover and transfer to the oven.
5. Cook for about 3 hours, or until the pork is very tender and shreds easily with a fork. Shred the pork in the pot with the juices.
6. For a crispy finish, spread the shredded pork on a baking sheet and broil for a few minutes until the edges are golden and crispy.
7. Serve the carnitas with a side of low-carb tortillas or over a bed of lettuce for a complete diabetic-friendly meal.

Nutritional Information. Per serving: 220 calories, 30g protein, 5g carbohydrates, 9g fat, 1g fiber, 75mg cholesterol, 300mg sodium, 500mg potassium.

This Pork Carnitas recipe is designed for diabetics, utilizing lean cuts of pork and cooking in a flavorful, citrus-infused low-sodium broth to keep it juicy and tender. The use of fresh ingredients and the absence of sugary sauces align with a diabetic-friendly diet, emphasizing proteins and healthy fats while minimizing carbohydrates and sugars. This dish offers a satisfying and nutritious option for anyone looking to enjoy traditional flavors more healthily.

BAKED HAM

Yield: 6 servings | Prep time: 15 minutes | Cook time: 2 hours

Ingredients:

3 lbs boneless ham (low-sodium)	1 tablespoon apple cider vinegar	1/2 teaspoon ground cinnamon
2 tablespoons Dijon mustard	2 teaspoons stevia (or another sugar substitute)	1/4 teaspoon ground cloves
1 tablespoon olive oil		1/2 cup water

Directions:

1. Preheat the oven to 325°F (165°C). Place the ham in a roasting pan and score the surface in a diamond pattern.

2. In a small bowl, mix the Dijon mustard, apple cider vinegar, olive oil, stevia, cinnamon, and cloves to create a diabetic-friendly glaze.

3. Brush half of the glaze evenly over the ham. Pour the water into the bottom of the roasting pan to help keep the ham moist during cooking.

4. Cover the ham with foil and bake for about 1.5 hours. Halfway through the cooking time, remove the foil and brush the ham with the remaining glaze.

5. Continue baking, uncovered, for the remaining time, or until the internal temperature reaches 140°F (60°C).

6. Let the ham rest for 10 minutes before slicing. Serve with a side of steamed green vegetables for a complete meal.

Nutritional Information. Per serving: 240 calories, 30g protein, 3g carbohydrates, 12g fat, 0g fiber, 85mg cholesterol, 1,200mg sodium, 400mg potassium.

This Baked Ham recipe is designed with diabetics in mind, carefully considering portion sizes and sugar content in the glaze. By using a sugar substitute and spices for flavor, the recipe reduces unnecessary sugar intake while still providing a delicious and festive dish. Watching the sodium content in the ham and opting for a low-sodium variety when available can also help manage blood pressure, making this dish a thoughtful option for those managing diabetes.

PORK AND VEGETABLES STIR-FRY

Yield: 4 servings | Prep time: 15 minutes | Cook time: 20 minutes

Ingredients:

1 lb lean pork loin, thinly sliced	1 cup snap peas	1 tablespoon apple cider vinegar
2 tablespoons olive oil	1 medium carrot, sliced thinly	1 teaspoon sesame oil
2 cups broccoli florets	2 cloves garlic, minced	Salt and pepper to taste
1 red bell pepper, sliced into strips	1 tablespoon grated ginger	Optional: sesame seeds for garnish
	1/4 cup low-sodium soy sauce	

Directions:

1. Heat 1 tablespoon of olive oil in a large skillet or wok over medium-high heat. Add the pork slices and stir-fry until they are browned and cooked through about 5-7 minutes. Remove the pork from the skillet and set aside.

2. In the same skillet, add the remaining tablespoon of olive oil. Add the broccoli, bell pepper, snap peas, carrot, garlic, and ginger. Stir-fry the vegetables until they are just tender, about 5-8 minutes.

3. In a small bowl, whisk together the low-sodium soy sauce, apple cider vinegar, and sesame oil. Add the cooked pork back to the skillet with the vegetables. Pour the sauce over the pork and vegetables, stirring to combine. Cook for another 2-3 minutes, allowing the sauce to thicken slightly.

4. Season with salt and pepper to taste. Serve the stir-fry hot, garnished with sesame seeds if desired.

Nutritional Information. Per serving: 240 calories, 25g protein, 10g carbohydrates, 11g fat, 3g fiber, 60mg cholesterol, 400mg sodium, 600mg potassium.

This Pork and vegetable stir-fry recipe is designed to be diabetic-friendly, emphasizing lean protein, a high content of fiber-rich vegetables, and the use of low-sodium ingredients. The combination of flavors from fresh garlic, ginger, and a hint of sesame oil provides a satisfying taste without the need for high-sugar sauces or marinades, making it a balanced meal option for managing blood sugar levels effectively.

PORK AND BEAN SOUP

Yield: 6 servings | Prep time: 15 minutes | Cook time: 1 hour

Ingredients:

1 lb lean pork tenderloin, cut into 1-inch cubes	1 can (15 ounces) low-sodium black beans, rinsed and drained	4 cups low-sodium chicken broth
1 tablespoon olive oil		1 can (14.5 ounces) diced tomatoes, no salt added
1 onion, diced	1 can (15 ounces) low-sodium cannellini beans, rinsed and drained	1 teaspoon dried oregano
2 cloves garlic, minced		Salt and pepper to taste
2 carrots, diced		2 cups water (adjust thickness)
2 stalks celery, diced	1 teaspoon dried thyme	

Directions:

1. Heat olive oil in a large pot over medium-high heat. Add the pork cubes and brown on all sides, about 5 minutes. Remove pork and set aside.

2. In the same pot, add onion, garlic, carrots, and celery. Sauté until vegetables are softened, about 5 minutes.

3. Return the pork to the pot. Add the black beans, cannellini beans, chicken broth, diced tomatoes, thyme, oregano, salt, and pepper. Stir well to combine.

4. Bring the mixture to a boil, then reduce heat to low, cover, and simmer for about 45 minutes to 1 hour, until the pork is tender.

5. Adjust the seasoning as needed and add water to reach your preferred soup consistency. Serve hot.

Nutritional Information. Per serving: 280 calories, 28g protein, 30g carbohydrates, 6g fat, 8g fiber, 45mg cholesterol, 300mg sodium, 800mg potassium.

This Pork and Bean Soup recipe provides a balanced and nutritious option for diabetics, focusing on lean protein from pork tenderloin and high fiber from beans, which can help manage blood sugar levels. The use of low-sodium ingredients helps maintain a healthy blood pressure, making this dish not only delicious but also heart-healthy. It's a comforting and filling meal that's perfect for any time of year.

PORK STIR-FRY

Yield: 4 servings | Prep time: 15 minutes | Cook time: 10 minutes

Ingredients:

1 lb lean pork loin, thinly sliced	1 cup snap peas	1/4 cup low-sodium soy sauce
2 tablespoons olive oil	1 carrot, julienned	2 tablespoons rice vinegar
2 cups broccoli florets	2 cloves garlic, minced	1 teaspoon sesame oil
1 red bell pepper, julienned	1 tablespoon grated ginger	Salt and pepper to taste

Directions:

1. Heat 1 tablespoon of olive oil in a large skillet or wok over medium-high heat. Add the pork slices and stir-fry until they are fully cooked and no longer pink, about 3-4 minutes. Remove the pork from the skillet and set aside.

2. Add the remaining tablespoon of olive oil to the skillet. Add the broccoli, bell pepper, snap peas, carrot, garlic, and ginger. Stir-fry the vegetables until they are just tender, about 5 minutes.

3. In a small bowl, whisk together the low-sodium soy sauce, rice vinegar, and sesame oil. Add the cooked pork back to the skillet along with the sauce. Stir well to combine and cook for an additional 2 minutes, allowing the flavors to meld together.

4. Season with salt and pepper to taste. Serve the stir-fry hot, ideally with a side of brown rice or quinoa for a complete meal.

Nutritional Information. Per serving: Approximately 250 calories, 25g protein, 10g carbohydrates, 11g fat, 3g fiber, 60mg cholesterol, 400mg sodium, 500mg potassium.

This Stir-Fry with Pork recipe is designed to be diabetic-friendly, focusing on lean protein from pork loin and a variety of vegetables rich in fiber, vitamins, and minerals. The low-sodium soy sauce and other seasonings provide flavor without adding excessive sodium or sugar, making it a balanced and nutritious option for managing diabetes.

PORK AND CABBAGE STIR-FRY

Yield: 4 servings | Prep time: 15 minutes | Cook time: 20 minutes

Ingredients:

1 pound pork tenderloin, thinly sliced	1 tablespoon fresh ginger, minced	1 teaspoon sesame oil
4 cups shredded cabbage	2 tablespoons low-sodium soy sauce	Salt and pepper to taste
1 tablespoon olive oil	1 tablespoon rice vinegar	2 green onions, sliced (for garnish)
2 cloves garlic, minced		1 teaspoon sesame seeds

Directions:

1. Heat the olive oil in a large skillet or wok over medium-high heat. Add the pork slices and stir-fry until they are no longer pink, about 5-7 minutes. Remove pork from the skillet and set aside.

2. In the same skillet, add garlic and ginger, and stir-fry for about 1 minute or until fragrant. Add the shredded cabbage and cook until it starts to wilt about 5 minutes.

3. Return the pork to the skillet. Add soy sauce, rice vinegar, and sesame oil. Stir well to combine. Season with salt and pepper to taste. Cook for another 2-3 minutes, or until everything is heated through.

4. Garnish with green onions and sesame seeds before serving.

Nutritional Information. Per serving: 220 calories, 25g protein, 8g carbohydrates, 10g fat, 3g fiber, 60mg cholesterol, 320mg sodium, 500mg potassium.

This Pork and Cabbage Stir-Fry recipe is a fast, flavorful, and nutritious option perfect for those managing diabetes. It combines lean protein from the pork with the health benefits of cabbage, all seasoned with a light and savory sauce. It's an ideal dish for a healthy, balanced diet, providing good amounts of protein and fiber while keeping the carbohydrate content low.

GRILLED LAMB CHOPS

Yield: 4 servings | Prep time: 15 minutes (plus marinating time) | Cook time: 10 minutes

Ingredients:

8 lamb chops, trimmed of excess fat	2 cloves garlic, minced	1 teaspoon thyme, chopped
2 tablespoons olive oil	1 teaspoon rosemary, chopped	Juice of 1 lemon
		Salt and pepper to taste

Directions:

1. In a small bowl, combine olive oil, garlic, rosemary, thyme, lemon juice, salt, and pepper to make the marinade.

2. Place lamb chops in a shallow dish or resealable plastic bag. Pour the marinade over the chops, ensuring they are well coated. Refrigerate and marinate for at least 2 hours, or overnight for best results.

3. Preheat the grill to medium-high heat. Remove lamb chops from the marinade, letting excess drip off. Discard the remaining marinade.

4. Grill lamb chops for 4-5 minutes per side for medium-rare, or until desired doneness.

5. Let the chops rest for a few minutes before serving to allow juices to redistribute.

Nutritional Information. Per serving: 310 calories, 28g protein, 0g carbohydrates, 22g fat, 0g fiber, 85mg cholesterol, 200mg sodium, 300mg potassium.

These Grilled Lamb Chops are designed with the dietary needs of diabetics in mind, focusing on high-quality protein and healthy fats while minimizing carbohydrates. The use of fresh herbs and lemon juice for flavoring reduces the need for added salts and sugars, making it a flavorful yet balanced option suitable for a diabetic diet.

HERB-CRUSTED LAMB RACK

Yield: 4 servings | Prep time: 20 minutes | Cook time: 25 minutes

Ingredients:

1 rack of lamb (about 1.5 to 2 lbs), trimmed of excess fat 2 tablespoons olive oil	2 cloves garlic, minced 2 tablespoons fresh rosemary, finely chopped Salt and pepper to taste	2 tablespoons fresh thyme, finely chopped 1 tablespoon Dijon mustard 2 tablespoons almond flour

Directions:

1. Preheat the oven to 400°F (200°C). Season the rack of lamb with salt and pepper. Heat 1 tablespoon of olive oil in a large skillet over medium-high heat. Add the lamb, fat side down, and sear until golden brown, about 3-4 minutes.

2. In a small bowl, mix the garlic, rosemary, thyme, and the remaining olive oil to form a paste. Set aside.

3. Once the lamb is seared, remove it from the skillet and let it cool slightly. Brush the Dijon mustard over the fat side of the lamb, then press the herb paste onto the mustard layer. Sprinkle the almond flour over the herb paste to form a crust.

4. Place the lamb rack on a roasting pan, crust side up. Roast in the preheated oven for 20-25 minutes for medium-rare, or until the desired doneness is reached. Use a meat thermometer to ensure accuracy (145°F for medium-rare).

5. Let the lamb rest for 10 minutes before carving into individual chops. This allows the juices to redistribute throughout the meat.

Nutritional Information. Per serving: 320 calories, 24g protein, 3g carbohydrates, 24g fat, 1g fiber, 85mg cholesterol, 200mg sodium, 350mg potassium.

This Herb-Crusted Lamb Rack recipe provides a flavorful and nutritious option for diabetics, focusing on lean protein and healthy fats. The use of fresh herbs and almond flour as a crust offers great taste without the added carbs found in traditional breadcrumbs coatings, making it a suitable choice for managing blood sugar levels.

LAMB KEBABS

Yield: 4 servings | Prep time: 20 minutes (plus marinating time) | Cook time: 10 minutes

Ingredients:

1 lb lamb loin, cut into 1-inch cubes 2 tablespoons olive oil 2 cloves garlic, minced 1 teaspoon ground cumin	1 teaspoon smoked paprika 1/2 teaspoon ground coriander Juice of 1 lemon	Salt and pepper to taste 1 red onion, cut into 1-inch pieces 1 bell pepper, cut into 1-inch pieces

Directions:

1. In a bowl, whisk together olive oil, garlic, cumin, paprika, coriander, lemon juice, salt, and pepper to create the marinade. Add the lamb cubes to the marinade, ensuring they are well coated. Cover and refrigerate for at least 2 hours, or overnight for the best flavor.

2. If using wooden skewers, soak them in water for at least 30 minutes before grilling to prevent burning.

3. Preheat the grill to medium-high heat. Thread the marinated lamb cubes onto skewers, alternating with pieces of red onion and bell pepper.

4. Grill the kebabs, turning occasionally, until the lamb is cooked to your desired level of doneness, about 8-10 minutes for medium-rare.

5. Let the kebabs rest for a few minutes before serving.

Nutritional Information. Per serving: 250 calories, 24g protein, 8g carbohydrates, 14g fat, 2g fiber, 65mg cholesterol, 200mg sodium, 500mg potassium.

These Diabetic-Friendly Lamb Kebabs are a perfect combination of lean protein and fresh vegetables, marinated in a delicious blend of spices and lemon juice. The recipe focuses on low-carb and healthy fats, ideal for managing blood sugar levels and supporting a diabetic diet. Enjoy a flavorful, nutritious meal that doesn't compromise your taste or health.

LEMON GARLIC LAMB STEAKS

Yield: 4 servings | Prep time: 10 minutes | Cook time: 12 minutes

Ingredients:

4 lamb steaks (about 6 ounces each) 2 tablespoons olive oil 2 cloves garlic, minced	Zest of 1 lemon 2 tablespoons lemon juice 1 teaspoon dried rosemary	1/2 teaspoon salt 1/4 teaspoon black pepper Fresh parsley, chopped (for garnish)

Directions:

1. In a small bowl, mix together olive oil, garlic, lemon zest, lemon juice, dried rosemary, salt, and pepper. Rub this mixture evenly over both sides of the lamb steaks.

2. Preheat a grill or grill pan over medium-high heat. Grill the lamb steaks for about 5-6 minutes per side for medium-rare, or until they reach your desired level of doneness.

3. Once cooked, remove the lamb steaks from the grill and let them rest for a few minutes. This helps retain their juices, making them more flavorful and tender.

4. Garnish the lamb steaks with fresh parsley before serving.

Nutritional Information. Per serving: 310 calories, 24g protein, 0g carbohydrates, 23g fat, 0g fiber, 85mg cholesterol, 340mg sodium, 305mg potassium.

This recipe offers a perfect blend of tangy lemon and aromatic garlic, paired with the rich, tender texture of lamb steaks, making it a luxurious yet easy-to-prepare dish for those managing diabetes or anyone in search of a healthful, flavorful meal. Its nutritional profile is carefully considered to support a balanced diet, ensuring you enjoy a delicious meal without compromising your health goals. The combination of high-quality protein, healthy fats, and low carbohydrates makes it an excellent choice for a satisfying and nutritious dinner.

BRAISED LAMB SHANKS

Yield: 4 servings | Prep time: 15 minutes | Cook time: 2 hours 30 minutes

Ingredients:

4 lamb shanks	2 cups low-sodium beef broth	1 teaspoon dried thyme
2 tablespoons olive oil		1 teaspoon dried rosemary
1 large onion, chopped	1 can (14.5 ounces) diced tomatoes, no-salt-added	1/2 teaspoon black pepper
2 cloves garlic, minced		1 bay leaf

Directions:

1. Preheat the oven to 325°F (165°C). In a large ovenproof pot, heat the olive oil over medium-high heat. Add the lamb shanks and brown them on all sides, then remove and set aside.

2. In the same pot, add the onion and garlic, cooking until softened, about 5 minutes. Return the lamb shanks to the pot. Add the beef broth, diced tomatoes (with their juice), thyme, rosemary, black pepper, and bay leaf.

3. Bring to a simmer, then cover and transfer the pot to the preheated oven. Braise the lamb shanks for about 2 to 2.5 hours, or until the meat is tender and falls off the bone.

4. Remove the bay leaf before serving. Skim off any excess fat from the sauce and adjust the seasoning if necessary.

Nutritional Information. Per serving: 410 calories, 48g protein, 8g carbohydrates, 20g fat, 2g fiber, 135mg cholesterol, 340mg sodium, 700mg potassium.

This recipe for Braised Lamb Shanks is designed to provide a hearty and nutritious meal that fits within a diabetic-friendly diet. The slow cooking process tenderizes the meat and melds the flavors of herbs and vegetables, creating a rich and satisfying dish without added sugars or high-sodium ingredients.

GREEK-STYLE LAMB GYROS

Yield: 4 servings | Prep time: 20 minutes | Cook time: 10 minutes

Ingredients:

1 lb lamb, thinly sliced	1 cucumber, diced	2 cloves garlic, minced
4 low-carb, whole wheat pita breads	2 tomatoes, diced	1 teaspoon dried oregano
1 cup Greek yogurt, unsweetened	1 small red onion, thinly sliced	1/2 teaspoon salt
	2 tablespoons olive oil	1/4 teaspoon black pepper
		1 tablespoon lemon juice

Directions:

1. In a bowl, combine olive oil, garlic, oregano, salt, pepper, and lemon juice. Add the lamb slices to the marinade, ensuring each piece is well-coated. Allow to marinate for at least 10 minutes.

2. Heat a grill pan or skillet over medium-high heat. Cook the lamb slices for about 3-4 minutes on each side, or until cooked to your preference.

3. Warm the pita breads in the oven or on a skillet for about a minute on each side to make them pliable.

4. Assemble the gyros by spreading Greek yogurt on each pita, adding a portion of the cooked lamb, and topping with cucumber, tomatoes, and red onion.

Nutritional Information. Per serving: 360 calories, 32g protein, 26g carbohydrates, 16g fat, 6g fiber, 75mg cholesterol, 420mg sodium, 560mg potassium.

This Greek-style Lamb Gyros recipe offers a delightful blend of flavors and textures, perfectly suited for a diabetic-friendly diet. With high-quality protein from lamb and Greek yogurt and a good balance of fiber from vegetables and whole wheat pita, it's designed to be both nutritious and satisfying without compromising blood sugar levels.

ROAST LEG OF LAMB

Yield: 6 servings | Prep time: 15 minutes | Cook time: 1 hour 30 minutes

Ingredients:

1 leg of lamb (about 5 pounds), bone-in 2 tablespoons olive oil 4 cloves garlic, minced	1 tablespoon fresh rosemary, chopped 1 tablespoon fresh thyme, chopped	1 teaspoon salt 1/2 teaspoon black pepper 1/2 cup low-sodium beef broth

Directions:

1. Preheat the oven to 350°F (175°C). In a small bowl, mix the olive oil, garlic, rosemary, thyme, salt, and pepper. Rub this mixture all over the leg of the lamb.

2. Place the lamb in a roasting pan and roast in the preheated oven for about 1 hour and 30 minutes, or until a meat thermometer inserted into the thickest part of the meat reads 145°F (63°C) for medium-rare.

3. Halfway through the cooking time, add the beef broth to the bottom of the roasting pan to keep the lamb moist and to prevent the drippings from burning.

4. Once cooked, remove the lamb from the oven and let it rest for 15 minutes before slicing. This allows the juices to redistribute throughout the meat, ensuring it is moist and flavorful.

Nutritional Information. Per serving: 410 calories, 48g protein, 0g carbohydrates, 24g fat, 0g fiber, 120mg cholesterol, 450mg sodium, 610mg potassium.

This Roast Leg of Lamb recipe is a classic dish made diabetic-friendly through careful consideration of ingredients and cooking methods, ensuring it is low in carbohydrates and high in protein. The use of fresh herbs and olive oil adds depth and flavor without adding unnecessary sugars or fats, making it an ideal choice for a nutritious and satisfying meal.

7. POULTRY

MEDITERRANEAN STUFFED CHICKEN BREAST

Yield: 4 servings | Prep time: 20 minutes | Cook time: 30 minutes

Ingredients:

4 boneless, skinless chicken breasts	1/4 cup crumbled feta cheese	1 teaspoon dried thyme
1/2 cup spinach, finely chopped	1/4 cup sun-dried tomatoes, chopped	1 teaspoon dried rosemary
	2 tablespoons olive oil	Salt and pepper to taste
		4 toothpicks

Directions:

1. Preheat the oven to 375°F. Using a sharp knife, cut a pocket into the side of each chicken breast.

2. In a bowl, mix the spinach, sun-dried tomatoes, and feta cheese. Stuff each chicken breast with the mixture, securing the opening with a toothpick.

3. Rub each chicken breast with olive oil and season with thyme, rosemary, salt, and pepper.

4. Place the stuffed chicken breasts on a greased baking tray. Bake for 30 minutes, or until the chicken is fully cooked (internal temperature reaches 165°F).

5. Let the chicken rest for 5 minutes before serving to allow the juices to redistribute.

Nutritional Information. Per serving: 260 calories, 31g protein, 3g carbohydrates, 14g fat, 1g fiber, 85mg cholesterol, 320mg sodium, 400mg potassium.

This Mediterranean Stuffed Chicken Breast recipe offers a delicious and nutritious meal, perfectly suited for diabetics. The combination of spinach, sun-dried tomatoes, and feta cheese provides a flavorful filling without adding excess carbohydrates. The chicken is not only a great source of lean protein but also helps in maintaining blood sugar levels. The herbs add a Mediterranean flair and additional antioxidants without extra calories.

CHICKEN AND VEGETABLE SKEWERS

Yield: 4 servings | Prep time: 20 minutes | Cook time: 15 minutes

Ingredients:

1 lb chicken breast, cut into 1-inch cubes	1 red onion, cut into 1-inch pieces	1 teaspoon dried oregano
2 bell peppers (any color), cut into 1-inch pieces	1 zucchini, sliced into 1/2-inch rounds	Salt and pepper to taste
2 tablespoons olive oil	1 teaspoon garlic powder	1 tablespoon lemon juice

Directions:

1. If using wooden skewers, soak them in water for at least 30 minutes to prevent burning.

2. Preheat your grill to medium-high heat or set your oven to broil.

3. In a large bowl, combine the olive oil, garlic powder, oregano, salt, pepper, and lemon juice. Add the chicken and vegetables to the bowl and toss to coat evenly.

4. Thread the chicken and vegetables onto the skewers, alternating between the chicken and vegetables.

5. Grill or broil the skewers for about 12-15 minutes, turning occasionally, until the chicken is cooked through and the vegetables are tender and slightly charred.

6. Serve the skewers hot, with a side of whole-grain rice or a salad for a complete diabetic-friendly meal.

Nutritional Information. Per serving: 250 calories, 26g protein, 10g carbohydrates, 11g fat, 2g fiber, 65mg cholesterol, 150mg sodium, 500mg potassium.

These Chicken and Vegetable Skewers are a great option for diabetics, focusing on lean protein, healthy fats, and a variety of vegetables. This dish is low in carbohydrates and high in fiber, making it suitable for managing blood sugar levels. The use of herbs and lemon juice for flavoring keeps the sodium content low, contributing to a heart-healthy and diabetic-friendly meal.

HERB-ROASTED TURKEY BREAST

Yield: 6 servings | Prep time: 15 minutes | Cook time: 90 minutes

Ingredients:

3 lb turkey breast, bone-in, skin-on	1 teaspoon garlic powder	1/2 teaspoon smoked paprika
	1 teaspoon dried rosemary	Salt and pepper to taste
2 tablespoons olive oil	1 teaspoon dried thyme	1/2 lemon, for juicing

Directions:

1. Preheat your oven to 350°F. In a small bowl, mix the olive oil, garlic powder, rosemary, thyme, smoked paprika, salt, and pepper to create a herb rub.

2. Pat the turkey breast dry with paper towels. Rub the herb mixture all over the turkey breast, ensuring it's well-coated. Squeeze lemon juice over the turkey for added flavor.

3. Place the turkey breast, skin side up, on a rack in a roasting pan. Tent loosely with aluminum foil to prevent excessive browning.

4. Roast in the preheated oven for about 90 minutes, or until the internal temperature reaches 165°F when measured with a meat thermometer inserted into the thickest part of the breast.

5. Let the turkey rest for 10 minutes before slicing to allow the juices to redistribute.

Nutritional Information. Per serving: 310 calories, 53g protein, 1g carbohydrates, 11g fat, 0g fiber, 125mg cholesterol, 200mg sodium, 450mg potassium.

This Herb-Roasted Turkey Breast recipe is a fantastic option for diabetics, offering a high-protein, low-carbohydrate meal that's flavorful and satisfying. The mix of herbs and spices adds a burst of flavor without the need for sugary sauces or marinades, making it a heart-healthy choice. The addition of lemon juice not only enhances taste but also helps in tenderizing the turkey, ensuring a juicy and delicious meal perfect for any occasion.

PARMESAN ALMOND CHICKEN CUTLETS

Yield: 4 servings | Prep time: 15 minutes | Cook time: 20 minutes

Ingredients:

4 skinless chicken breasts, pounded to 1/2 inch thickness 1/2 cup almond flour	1/4 cup grated Parmesan cheese 1 teaspoon garlic powder	1/2 teaspoon paprika Salt and pepper to taste 2 large eggs, beaten 2 tablespoons olive oil

Directions:

1. In a shallow dish, combine almond flour, grated Parmesan, garlic powder, paprika, salt, and pepper.

2. Place the beaten eggs in another shallow dish. Dip each chicken breast first into the egg, then coat with the almond flour mixture.

3. Heat olive oil in a large skillet over medium heat. Add the chicken cutlets and cook for about 10 minutes on each side, or until the chicken is golden brown and reaches an internal temperature of 165°F.

4. Serve the cutlets hot, garnished with a sprinkle of fresh parsley or a wedge of lemon if desired.

Nutritional Information. Per serving: 320 calories, 33g protein, 4g carbohydrates, 19g fat, 2g fiber, 145mg cholesterol, 320mg sodium, 300mg potassium.

This Parmesan Almond Chicken Cutlets recipe is a delicious and diabetic-friendly meal option. The use of almond flour and Parmesan cheese for the coating provides a lower carbohydrate alternative to traditional breadcrumbs, making it suitable for those managing their blood sugar levels. The cutlets are cooked in olive oil, adding healthy fats to the dish, while the spices ensure each bite is flavorful. This dish combines nutrition and taste, making it a perfect addition to any diabetic meal plan.

HERB-CRUSTED BAKED CHICKEN BREAST

Yield: 4 servings | Prep time: 10 minutes | Cook time: 25 minutes

Ingredients:

4 boneless, skinless chicken breasts (about 6 ounces each) 2 tablespoons olive oil	1 teaspoon garlic powder 1 teaspoon dried oregano 1 teaspoon dried basil	1/2 teaspoon paprika Salt and pepper to taste 1 lemon, sliced for garnish

Directions:

1. Preheat the oven to 375°F. Line a baking sheet with parchment paper or lightly grease it with cooking spray.

2. In a small bowl, combine the olive oil, garlic powder, oregano, basil, paprika, salt, and pepper. Rub this mixture evenly over both sides of each chicken breast.

3. Place the chicken breasts on the prepared baking sheet. If desired, place lemon slices on top for added flavor.

4. Bake in the preheated oven for 25 minutes, or until the chicken is cooked through and reaches an internal temperature of 165°F.

5. Let the chicken rest for 5 minutes before serving. This allows the juices to redistribute, keeping the chicken moist.

Nutritional Information. Per serving: 220 calories, 35g protein, 0g carbohydrates, 9g fat, 0g fiber, 95mg cholesterol, 200mg sodium, 300mg potassium.

This Herb-Crusted Baked Chicken Breast recipe is an ideal choice for diabetics, focusing on high protein and low carbohydrates to help manage blood sugar levels. The use of herbs and spices adds flavor without extra calories or sodium, making it a healthy and delicious option for anyone looking for a nutritious meal. The addition of lemon slices not only enhances the flavor but also provides a boost of vitamin C.

MAPLE-GLAZED TURKEY TENDERLOIN

Yield: 4 servings | Prep time: 10 minutes | Cook time: 35 minutes

Ingredients:

2 turkey tenderloins (about 1 lb each) 2 tablespoons olive oil	Salt and pepper to taste 1/4 cup sugar-free maple syrup	2 teaspoons Dijon mustard 1 teaspoon dried thyme 1 garlic clove, minced

Directions:

1. Preheat your oven to 375°F. Line a baking sheet with parchment paper or lightly grease it.

2. Rub the turkey tenderloins with olive oil, and season them with salt and pepper. Place them on the prepared baking sheet.

3. In a small bowl, whisk together the sugar-free maple syrup, Dijon mustard, thyme, and minced garlic to create the glaze.

4. Brush half of the glaze over the turkey tenderloins. Bake in the preheated oven for 15 minutes.

5. Remove the turkey from the oven, brush with the remaining glaze, and return to the oven. Continue baking for another 20 minutes, or until the internal temperature reaches 165°F.

6. Let the turkey rest for 5 minutes before slicing and serving.

Nutritional Information. Per serving: 280 calories, 35g protein, 5g carbohydrates, 12g fat, 0g fiber, 75mg cholesterol, 200mg sodium, 400mg potassium.

This Maple-Glazed Turkey Tenderloin recipe is a delightful and diabetic-friendly option that doesn't skimp on flavor. The sugar-free maple syrup and Dijon mustard provide a sweet and tangy taste, while the thyme and garlic add a savory depth. This dish is perfect for those looking to maintain balanced blood sugar levels while enjoying a satisfying and nutritious meal.

LEMON GARLIC ROASTED CHICKEN THIGHS

Yield: 4 servings | Prep time: 10 minutes | Cook time: 40 minutes

Ingredients:

8 bone-in, skin-on chicken thighs	4 garlic cloves, minced	1 teaspoon dried rosemary
2 tablespoons olive oil	1 lemon, juiced and zested	Salt and pepper to taste
	1 teaspoon dried thyme	

Directions:

1. Preheat your oven to 400°F. In a small bowl, combine olive oil, minced garlic, lemon juice and zest, thyme, rosemary, salt, and pepper to create a marinade.

2. Place chicken thighs in a large bowl and pour the marinade over them, making sure each thigh is well-coated. Let them marinate for at least 10 minutes.

3. Arrange the chicken thighs skin-side up on a large baking sheet. Roast in the preheated oven for about 40 minutes, or until the skin is crispy and a thermometer inserted into the thickest part of the thigh reads 165°F.

4. Let the chicken rest for 5 minutes before serving to allow the juices to redistribute.

Nutritional Information. Per serving: 410 calories, 35g protein, 2g carbohydrates, 30g fat, 0g fiber, 180mg cholesterol, 320mg sodium, 400mg potassium.

This Lemon Garlic Roasted Chicken Thighs recipe offers a delicious and health-conscious option for diabetics. The combination of lemon and garlic not only adds a burst of flavor but also tenderizes the chicken, ensuring each bite is juicy and satisfying. The use of olive oil adds healthy fats, while the herbs provide antioxidants without adding extra carbohydrates, making this dish perfectly balanced for a diabetic diet.

BAKED GOOSE LEGS WITH BAKED VEGETABLES

Yield: 4 servings | Prep time: 15 minutes | Cook time: 1 hour 30 minutes

Ingredients

4 goose legs (about 1 lb each)	1 teaspoon garlic powder	1 large red onion, cut into wedges
2 tablespoons olive oil	2 medium parsnips, peeled and cut into chunks	2 tablespoons balsamic vinegar
Salt and pepper to taste	1 small butternut squash, peeled, seeded, and cut into chunks	2 teaspoons sugar substitute (suitable for diabetics, like stevia)
1 teaspoon dried thyme		
4 medium carrots, peeled and cut into chunks		

Directions

1. Preheat the oven to 375°F. Rub the goose legs with 1 tablespoon of olive oil, then season with salt, pepper, thyme, and garlic powder. Place in a roasting pan.

2. In a large bowl, combine the carrots, parsnips, butternut squash, and red onion with the remaining olive oil, balsamic vinegar, and sugar substitute. Season with salt and pepper to taste and toss to coat evenly.

3. Arrange the vegetables around the goose legs in the roasting pan. Bake for approximately 1 hour and 30 minutes, or until the goose legs are cooked through and the vegetables are tender and caramelized, stirring the vegetables occasionally.

4. Let the goose legs rest for 10 minutes before serving with the roasted vegetables.

Nutritional Information. Per serving: 510 calories, 44g protein, 45g carbohydrates, 18g fat, 8g fiber, 150mg cholesterol, 320mg sodium, 1200mg potassium.

This recipe provides a hearty and nutritious meal with a good balance of protein, complex carbohydrates, and healthy fats, suitable for those managing diabetes. The use of sugar substitutes and natural sweetness from the vegetables enhances the flavor without adding excess sugar.

FRIED GOOSE BREAST WITH BERRY SAUCE

Yield: 4 servings | Prep time: 15 minutes | Cook time: 20 minutes

Ingredients:

4 goose breasts (about 6 oz each) 1/4 teaspoon of salt 1/4 teaspoon of black pepper 1/4 cup red wine vinegar 2 tablespoons olive oil	1 cup mixed berries (raspberries, blueberries, strawberries) 2 tablespoons of a diabetic-friendly sweetener (e.g., erythritol)	1 teaspoon fresh thyme, chopped 1 tablespoon cornstarch, dissolved in 2 tablespoons of water (optional, for thickening)

Directions:

1. Season the goose breasts with salt and pepper. In a large skillet, heat the olive oil over medium-high heat. Once hot, add the goose breasts skin-side down and cook for about 5 minutes until the skin is golden and crispy. Flip the breasts and cook for another 10-15 minutes or until they reach an internal temperature of 165°F. Remove from the skillet and let them rest.

2. In the same skillet, reduce the heat to medium. Add the mixed berries, red wine vinegar, and sweetener. Cook, stirring occasionally, until the berries start to break down and the sauce thickens slightly, about 5-7 minutes. For a thicker sauce, stir in the cornstarch mixture and simmer for another 2-3 minutes.

3. Slice the goose breasts and serve them with the berry sauce spooned over the top.

Nutritional Information. Per serving: 310 calories, 35g protein, 8g carbohydrates, 12g fat, 2g fiber, 85mg cholesterol, 320mg sodium, 350mg potassium.

This diabetic-friendly recipe balances rich, flavorful goose with a tangy and sweet berry sauce, providing a satisfying meal without compromising blood sugar levels. Using a sugar substitute and fresh berries adds natural sweetness and antioxidants, making it a healthful choice for those managing diabetes.

GRILLED QUAIL WITH CITRUS MARINADE

Yield: 4 servings | Prep time: 15 minutes (plus marinating time) | Cook time: 20 minutes

Ingredients

8 quail, cleaned and ready for grilling	2 tablespoons apple cider vinegar	1 tablespoon fresh thyme, chopped
1/4 cup olive oil	2 cloves garlic, minced	Salt and pepper to taste
Juice and zest of 1 orange	1 tablespoon fresh rosemary, chopped	Sugar substitute equivalent to 1 tablespoon of sugar
Juice and zest of 1 lemon		

Directions

1. In a large bowl, whisk together olive oil, orange juice and zest, lemon juice and zest, apple cider vinegar, minced garlic, rosemary, thyme, salt, pepper, and sugar substitute. Add the quail, ensuring they are thoroughly coated in the marinade. Cover and refrigerate for at least 2 hours, or overnight for the best flavor.

2. Preheat the grill to medium-high heat. Remove quail from the marinade, letting excess drip off. Grill the quail for about 10 minutes on each side, or until the internal temperature reaches 165°F and the skin is golden and crispy.

3. Let the quail rest for a few minutes before serving. Optionally, you can boil the remaining marinade for 5 minutes to serve as a sauce alongside the quail.

Nutritional Information. Per serving: 310 calories, 35g protein, 5g carbohydrates, 18g fat, 1g fiber, 105mg cholesterol, 75mg sodium, 350mg potassium.

This recipe combines the rich flavor of quail with a fresh and zesty citrus marinade, offering a delightful balance suitable for a diabetic diet. The use of sugar substitutes and healthy fats from olive oil make it a great choice for maintaining balanced blood sugar levels.

8. FISH AND SEAFOOD

LEMON HERB BAKED COD

Yield: 4 servings | Prep time: 10 minutes | Cook time: 20 minutes

Ingredients:

4 cod fillets (6 ounces each) 2 tablespoons olive oil	1 lemon, juiced and zested 2 garlic cloves, minced 1 teaspoon dried thyme	1 teaspoon dried parsley Salt to taste Pepper to taste

Directions:

1. Preheat your oven to 400°F. In a small bowl, mix together olive oil, lemon juice and zest, minced garlic, thyme, parsley, salt, and pepper to create a marinade.

2. Place the cod fillets in a baking dish. Pour the marinade evenly over the fillets, ensuring each piece is well-coated.

3. Bake in the preheated oven for 20 minutes, or until the fish flakes easily with a fork.

4. Serve immediately, garnishing with additional lemon slices or fresh parsley if desired.

Nutritional Information. Per serving: 190 calories, 23g protein, 1g carbohydrates, 10g fat, 0g fiber, 60mg cholesterol, 125mg sodium, 500mg potassium.

This Lemon Herb Baked Cod recipe is a simple, flavorful, and nutritious meal option for diabetics. The combination of lemon and herbs not only adds a light and refreshing flavor but also complements the delicate taste of the cod without adding unnecessary carbohydrates or fats. This dish is high in protein and low in calories, making it an ideal choice for managing blood sugar levels while providing essential nutrients.

DILL AND LEMON-POACHED TROUT

Yield: 4 servings | Prep time: 5 minutes | Cook time: 10 minutes

Ingredients:

4 trout fillets (6 ounces each) 4 cups of water 1 lemon, thinly sliced	1/4 cup fresh dill, plus extra for garnish 2 bay leaves	1 teaspoon whole black peppercorns 1 teaspoon salt

Directions:

1. In a large skillet or pot, bring the water to a gentle simmer. Add the lemon slices, fresh dill, bay leaves, black peppercorns, and salt to the water to create a flavorful poaching liquid.

2. Carefully place the trout fillets in the simmering water, ensuring they are fully submerged. Add more water if necessary.

3. Poach the trout over low heat for about 10 minutes, or until the fish is opaque and flakes easily with a fork. The water should barely simmer to keep the fish tender.

4. Use a slotted spoon to remove the trout from the water. Serve the fillets on plates, garnished with additional dill and lemon slices as desired.

Nutritional Information. Per serving: 145 calories, 23g protein, 0g carbohydrates, 5g fat, 0g fiber, 67mg cholesterol, 600mg sodium, 380mg potassium.

This Dill and Lemon Poached Trout recipe is another excellent choice for diabetics, providing a high-protein, low-fat, and carb-free meal option. The combination of lemon and dill not only imparts a refreshing flavor to the trout but also offers health benefits, including aiding digestion and providing vitamin C. This method of cooking ensures the fish remains moist and flavorful, making it a satisfying dish for any meal.

STEAMED TILAPIA WITH LEMON AND HERBS

Yield: 4 servings | Prep time: 5 minutes | Cook time: 12 minutes

Ingredients:

4 tilapia fillets (6 ounces each) 1 lemon, thinly sliced 2 cloves garlic, minced	2 tablespoons fresh dill, chopped 1/4 cup water or white wine	2 tablespoons fresh parsley, chopped Salt and pepper to taste

Directions:

1. Season the tilapia fillets with salt and pepper. Arrange half of the lemon slices on the bottom of a steaming basket or tray.

2. Place the tilapia on top of the lemon slices. Sprinkle the minced garlic, dill, and parsley evenly over the fillets. Top with the remaining lemon slices.

3. Pour water or white wine into the bottom of a pot, ensuring that the water level does not touch the bottom of the steamer basket. Bring the liquid to a simmer.

4. Place the steaming basket over the simmering water, cover the pot, and steam for about 12 minutes or until the fish flakes easily with a fork.

5. Carefully remove the steamed tilapia and serve immediately, garnished with additional fresh herbs if desired.

Nutritional Information. Per serving: 125 calories, 26g protein, 1g carbohydrates, 2g fat, 0g fiber, 55mg cholesterol, 60mg sodium, 400mg potassium.

This Steamed Tilapia with Lemon and Herbs recipe offers a light, refreshing, and nutritious meal option for diabetics. The combination of lemon and fresh herbs not only infuses the fish with flavor but also provides antioxidants and vitamins. Steaming the fish ensures that it remains moist and tender while keeping the added fats to a minimum, making it an excellent choice for anyone managing blood sugar levels or looking for a heart-healthy diet. The simplicity of the recipe highlights the natural flavors of the ingredients, making it a delightful dish suitable for any occasion.

SPICY PAPRIKA BAKED SALMON

Yield: 4 servings | Prep time: 10 minutes | Cook time: 15 minutes

Ingredients:

4 salmon fillets (6 ounces each) 2 tablespoons olive oil	2 teaspoons smoked paprika 1/2 teaspoon cayenne pepper (adjust to taste)	1 teaspoon garlic powder Salt and pepper to taste 1 lemon, sliced for garnish

Directions:

1. Preheat your oven to 425°F. In a small bowl, combine the olive oil, smoked paprika, garlic powder, cayenne pepper, salt, and pepper to create a spice rub.

2. Lay the salmon fillets on a baking sheet lined with parchment paper. Rub the spice mixture evenly over the top of each fillet.

3. Bake in the preheated oven for 15 minutes, or until the salmon is cooked through and flakes easily with a fork.

4. Serve immediately, garnished with lemon slices to add a refreshing zest.

Nutritional Information. Per serving: 280 calories, 25g protein, 0g carbohydrates, 20g fat, 0g fiber, 65mg cholesterol, 75mg sodium, 600mg potassium.

This Spicy Paprika Baked Salmon recipe offers a rich, smoky flavor with a hint of heat, making it a perfect main dish for diabetics looking for a tasty yet healthy meal. The high-quality proteins and healthy fats in salmon support heart health and blood sugar management. The bold spices add depth and excitement to the dish without contributing additional carbs, ensuring a diabetic-friendly meal that doesn't compromise on flavor.

GINGER-POACHED TILAPIA

Yield: 4 servings | Prep time: 5 minutes | Cook time: 15 minutes

Ingredients:

4 tilapia fillets (6 ounces each)	1/4 cup fresh ginger, thinly sliced	1 teaspoon salt
4 cups water	2 green onions, cut into 2-inch pieces	1/2 lemon, sliced (plus extra for serving)
2 garlic cloves, smashed		Fresh parsley for garnish

Directions:

1. In a large pot, bring water to a simmer. Add the ginger, garlic, green onions, salt, and lemon slices. Simmer for 5 minutes to infuse the water with flavors.

2. Gently add the tilapia fillets to the pot. Make sure the water covers the fish. If necessary, add more water.

3. Simmer gently for about 10 minutes, or until the fish is cooked through and flakes easily with a fork. Avoid boiling vigorously to keep the fish from falling apart.

4. Use a slotted spoon to transfer the fish to plates. Garnish with fresh parsley and serve with extra lemon slices on the side.

Nutritional Information. Per serving: 110 calories, 23g protein, 0g carbohydrates, 2g fat, 0g fiber, 55mg cholesterol, 590mg sodium, 350mg potassium.

This Ginger Poached Tilapia recipe is a simple, healthy, and delicious option for diabetics. The gentle poaching method preserves the delicate flavor of the tilapia while infusing it with the aromatic qualities of ginger, garlic, and lemon. This dish is low in calories and fat but high in protein, making it an excellent choice for those managing diabetes. The absence of carbohydrates ensures that it won't spike blood sugar levels, offering a nutritious meal that also supports overall health.

STEAMED GINGER SOY HADDOCK

Yield: 4 servings | Prep time: 10 minutes | Cook time: 15 minutes

Ingredients:

4 haddock fillets (6 ounces each)	2 tablespoons sesame oil	4 green onions, sliced
	2 inches fresh ginger, grated	1 bell pepper, thinly sliced
1/4 cup soy sauce (low sodium)	4 garlic cloves, minced	Salt and pepper to taste

Directions:

1. In a small bowl, mix together soy sauce, sesame oil, grated ginger, and minced garlic to create the marinade.

2. Season the haddock fillets with a little salt and pepper, then place them in a single layer in a steaming basket. Spread the green onions and bell pepper slices over the top of the fish.

3. Pour the marinade evenly over the fish and vegetables.

4. Set the steaming basket over a pot of boiling water, cover, and steam for about 15 minutes, or until the fish flakes easily with a fork and the vegetables are tender.

5. Serve immediately, garnishing with additional green onions or sesame seeds if desired.

Nutritional Information. Per serving: 200 calories, 27g protein, 5g carbohydrates, 8g fat, 1g fiber, 60mg cholesterol, 480mg sodium, 500mg potassium.

This Steamed Ginger Soy Haddock recipe is a flavorful, nutritious, and diabetic-friendly meal. The fish is steamed with fresh ginger, garlic, and vegetables, making it rich in vitamins and minerals while keeping the calorie and fat content low. The use of low-sodium soy sauce and sesame oil adds depth and a healthy dose of omega-3 fatty acids without overwhelming the palate with salt, making it an ideal choice for those managing diabetes and looking for heart-healthy options.

GRILLED SHRIMP SKEWERS WITH VEGETABLE KABOBS

Yield: 4 servings | Prep time: 20 minutes | Cook time: 10 minutes

Ingredients

1 lb large shrimp, peeled and deveined	2 bell peppers (any color), cut into 1-inch pieces	2 cloves garlic, minced
2 zucchinis, cut into 1/2-inch slices	1 large red onion, cut into wedges	1 teaspoon dried oregano
2 tablespoons olive oil	Juice of 1 lemon	Salt and pepper to taste
		8 skewers (if wooden, soak in water before use)

Directions

1. In a large bowl, combine olive oil, lemon juice, minced garlic, oregano, salt, and pepper. Add the shrimp and vegetables to the bowl and toss to coat evenly. Let marinate for 15 minutes.

2. Thread the marinated shrimp and vegetables onto the skewers, alternating between shrimp and vegetables.

3. Preheat the grill to medium-high heat. Grill the skewers for 2-3 minutes on each side, or until the shrimp are opaque and the vegetables are tender and slightly charred.

4. Serve immediately, optionally with a side of whole grain rice or a fresh salad for a complete meal.

Nutritional Information. Per serving: 220 calories, 24g protein, 12g carbohydrates, 9g fat, 3g fiber, 180mg cholesterol, 200mg sodium, 400mg potassium.

This recipe is an excellent choice for diabetics, offering a high-protein, low-carbohydrate meal with healthy fats and fiber to help manage blood sugar levels. The vibrant mix of vegetables provides essential vitamins and minerals, making it a nutritious and flavorful option for any meal.

SEAFOOD STIR-FRY

Yield: 4 servings | Prep time: 15 minutes | Cook time: 10 minutes

Ingredients

1 lb mixed seafood (shrimp, scallops, squid), peeled and deveined	1 carrot, thinly sliced	1 teaspoon sugar substitute
	2 garlic cloves, minced	Salt and pepper to taste
	1 tablespoon ginger, minced	1 tablespoon sesame oil
2 tablespoons olive oil	1/4 cup low-sodium soy sauce	2 green onions, chopped, for garnish
1 cup broccoli florets		
1 red bell pepper, sliced	2 tablespoons oyster sauce	Sesame seeds, for garnish

Directions

1. Heat olive oil in a large skillet or wok over medium-high heat. Add the garlic and ginger, and stir-fry for 30 seconds until fragrant.

2. Add the mixed seafood to the skillet and stir-fry for 2-3 minutes until just cooked through. Remove seafood from the skillet and set aside.

3. In the same skillet, add the broccoli, bell pepper, and carrot. Stir-fry for 4-5 minutes until the vegetables are tender-crisp.

4. Return the seafood to the skillet. Add the soy sauce, oyster sauce, sugar substitute, and season with salt and pepper. Stir well to combine and heat through, about 2 minutes. Drizzle with sesame oil and toss to combine.

5. Serve immediately, garnished with green onions and sesame seeds.

Nutritional Information. Per serving: 230 calories, 25g protein, 10g carbohydrates, 11g fat, 2g fiber, 175mg cholesterol, 500mg sodium, 350mg potassium.

This seafood stir-fry offers a high-protein, low-carbohydrate meal that's rich in omega-3 fatty acids and essential nutrients, making it a great option for diabetics. The combination of colorful vegetables adds vitamins and fiber, while the use of low-sodium soy sauce and sugar substitute keeps it diabetic-friendly.

STEAMED MUSSELS IN TOMATO AND HERB BROTH

Yield: 4 servings | Prep time: 15 minutes | Cook time: 10 minutes

Ingredients

2 lbs fresh mussels, cleaned and debearded 1 tablespoon olive oil 1/4 cup dry white wine (optional, can be replaced with extra broth for non-alcoholic version)	3 garlic cloves, minced 1 small onion, finely chopped 1 can (14 oz) diced tomatoes, no salt added 1/2 cup low-sodium vegetable broth	1 teaspoon sugar substitute (suitable for diabetics) 1 tablespoon fresh basil, chopped 1 tablespoon fresh parsley, chopped Salt and pepper to taste

Directions

1. Heat olive oil in a large pot over medium heat. Add the garlic and onion, and sauté until softened, about 2-3 minutes.

2. Add the diced tomatoes, vegetable broth, white wine (if using), and sugar substitute to the pot. Bring to a simmer and cook for 5 minutes, allowing the flavors to meld.

3. Add the mussels to the pot, cover, and steam until all mussels have opened, about 5 minutes. Discard any mussels that do not open.

4. Stir in the chopped basil and parsley, and season with salt and pepper to taste. Serve immediately.

Nutritional Information. Per serving: 210 calories, 22g protein, 12g carbohydrates, 7g fat, 1g fiber, 50mg cholesterol, 340mg sodium, 500mg potassium.

This recipe offers a flavorful and nutritious option for diabetics, focusing on high-quality protein and low carbohydrates. The use of fresh herbs and tomato-based broth adds vitamins and antioxidants while keeping the overall dish light and suitable for a diabetic diet.

MUSSELS WITH GARLIC AND WHITE WINE SAUCE

Yield: 4 servings | Prep time: 20 minutes | Cook time: 10 minutes

Ingredients

2 lbs fresh mussels, cleaned and debearded	4 garlic cloves, minced	2 tablespoons fresh parsley, chopped
2 tablespoons olive oil	1 cup dry white wine	Salt and pepper to taste
1/2 cup finely chopped shallots	1 tablespoon unsalted butter	Lemon wedges for serving
	1/2 cup low-sodium chicken broth	

Directions

1. In a large pot, heat olive oil over medium heat. Add garlic and shallots, and sauté until soft and fragrant, about 2-3 minutes.

2. Pour in the white wine and chicken broth, and bring to a simmer. Add the mussels, cover the pot, and cook until the mussels have opened, about 5-7 minutes. Discard any mussels that do not open.

3. Using a slotted spoon, transfer the mussels to serving bowls. Add butter to the sauce in the pot, stir until melted, and season with salt and pepper.

4. Pour the sauce over the mussels, sprinkle with fresh parsley, and serve with lemon wedges on the side.

Nutritional Information. Per serving: 295 calories, 24g protein, 15g carbohydrates, 10g fat, 0g fiber, 48mg cholesterol, 430mg sodium, 380mg potassium.

This delicious recipe for Mussels with Garlic and White Wine Sauce is designed with diabetics in mind, featuring low-carbohydrate content and a focus on lean protein and healthy fats. The addition of fresh herbs and the use of dry white wine create a flavorful, aromatic sauce without adding excess sugar or calories, making it a perfect choice for a diabetic-friendly meal.

THAI-INSPIRED COCONUT CURRY MUSSELS

Yield: 4 servings | Prep time: 15 minutes | Cook time: 15 minutes

Ingredients

2 lbs fresh mussels, cleaned and debearded	1 tablespoon fresh ginger, grated	1 teaspoon sugar substitute (like stevia)
1 tablespoon coconut oil	1 tablespoon red curry paste	Juice of 1 lime
1 small onion, finely chopped	1 can (14 oz) light coconut milk	1/4 cup fresh cilantro, chopped
2 garlic cloves, minced	1 tablespoon fish sauce	Salt to taste

Directions

1. In a large pot, heat coconut oil over medium heat. Add onion, garlic, and ginger, sautéing until soft and fragrant, about 3-5 minutes.

2. Stir in the red curry paste and cook for 1 minute. Pour in the coconut milk, fish sauce, and sugar substitute, bringing the mixture to a simmer.

3. Add the mussels to the pot, cover, and cook until the mussels have opened, about 5-8 minutes. Discard any mussels that do not open.

4. Stir in lime juice and half of the chopped cilantro. Season with salt to taste.

5. Serve hot, garnished with the remaining cilantro.

Nutritional Information. Per serving: 310 calories, 25g protein, 10g carbohydrates, 18g fat, 0g fiber, 50mg cholesterol, 700mg sodium, 400mg potassium.

This Thai-Inspired Coconut Curry Mussels recipe offers a flavorful and nutritious option for diabetics, focusing on lean protein, healthy fats from coconut milk, and low carbohydrates. The use of a sugar substitute and natural lime juice provides sweetness and acidity without adding excess sugar, making it a well-balanced choice for maintaining stable blood sugar levels.

BAKED LEMON-GARLIC SCALLOPS

Yield: 4 servings | Prep time: 10 minutes | Cook time: 15 minutes

Ingredients

1 1/2 lbs large sea scallops 3 tablespoons olive oil Juice and zest of 1 lemon	3 cloves garlic, minced 1 tablespoon fresh parsley, chopped	Salt and pepper to taste Lemon slices, for garnish

Directions

1. Preheat the oven to 400°F. In a small bowl, mix olive oil, lemon juice and zest, minced garlic, parsley, salt, and pepper.

2. Arrange the scallops in a single layer in a baking dish. Drizzle the lemon-garlic mixture over the scallops, ensuring they are evenly coated.

3. Bake in the preheated oven for 12-15 minutes, or until the scallops are opaque and cooked through.

4. Serve immediately, garnished with lemon slices and additional chopped parsley if desired.

Nutritional Information. Per serving: 220 calories, 23g protein, 7g carbohydrates, 10g fat, 0g fiber, 55mg cholesterol, 320mg sodium, 500mg potassium.

This baked lemon-garlic scallops recipe offers a light, flavorful, and nutritious option for diabetics, focusing on high-quality protein, healthy fats, and low carbohydrates. The absence of fiber is typical for seafood dishes, but pairing this meal with a side of vegetables can balance the dietary fiber intake.

9. STEWS AND SOUPS

BEEF AND BARLEY STEW

Yield: 4 servings | Prep time: 20 minutes | Cook time: 1 hour 30 minutes

Ingredients:

1 pound lean beef stew meat, cut into 1-inch pieces	1 cup water	2 cloves garlic, minced
1 tablespoon olive oil	3/4 cup barley	1 teaspoon dried thyme
4 cups low-sodium beef broth	2 carrots, diced	1/2 teaspoon black pepper
	2 celery stalks, diced	1 bay leaf
	1 onion, diced	

Directions:

1. Heat olive oil in a large pot over medium-high heat. Brown the beef on all sides.

2. Add the beef broth, water, barley, carrots, celery, onion, garlic, thyme, black pepper, and bay leaf to the pot. Bring to a boil.

3. Reduce heat to low, cover, and simmer for about 1 hour and 20 minutes, or until the beef is tender and the barley is fully cooked.

4. Discard the bay leaf before serving. Ensure the stew is well-seasoned, adjusting with salt and pepper to taste.

Nutritional Information. Per serving: 350 calories, 24g protein, 40g carbohydrates, 10g fat, 8g fiber, 55mg cholesterol, 200mg sodium, 600mg potassium.

This Beef and Barley Stew is a hearty, nutritious meal, perfect for those managing diabetes. The combination of lean beef and barley provides a good balance of protein and fiber, promoting fullness and blood sugar control. Low in sodium and fat, it supports heart health, making it a great option for a cozy, comforting dinner.

RABBIT STEW

Yield: 4 servings | Prep time: 20 minutes | Cook time: 1 hour 45 minutes

Ingredients:

1 (3-pound) rabbit, cut into pieces	2 celery stalks, sliced	1 can (14.5 ounces) diced tomatoes, no-salt-added
2 tablespoons olive oil	1 cup sliced mushrooms	1 bay leaf
1 large onion, chopped	1 cup dry red wine	Salt and pepper to taste
2 cloves garlic, minced	2 cups low-sodium chicken broth	2 tablespoons fresh parsley, chopped (for garnish)
2 carrots, peeled and sliced	1 teaspoon dried thyme	

Directions:

1. Heat the olive oil in a large pot over medium-high heat. Add the rabbit pieces and brown on all sides, then remove and set aside.

2. In the same pot, add the onion, garlic, carrots, celery, and mushrooms. Cook until the vegetables are softened, about 5-7 minutes.

3. Return the rabbit to the pot. Add the red wine, chicken broth, diced tomatoes, thyme, bay leaf, salt, and pepper. Bring to a boil, then reduce the heat to low, cover, and simmer for 1 hour and 30 minutes, or until the rabbit is tender.

4. Remove the bay leaf and adjust the seasoning as needed. Garnish with fresh parsley before serving.

Nutritional Information. Per serving: 350 calories, 45g protein, 15g carbohydrates, 12g fat, 3g fiber, 105mg cholesterol, 300mg sodium, 800mg potassium.

This Rabbit Stew recipe is a hearty, nutritious meal that's perfect for individuals managing diabetes. It's rich in protein, low in carbohydrates, and includes a variety of vegetables, making it balanced and flavorful. The addition of red wine and herbs lends depth to the stew, creating a comforting dish that's ideal for a cozy dinner.

HEARTY VEGETABLE AND LENTIL STEW

Yield: 4 servings | Prep time: 15 minutes | Cook time: 45 minutes

Ingredients:

1 tablespoon olive oil	1 cup dried lentils, rinsed	1 teaspoon dried thyme
1 large onion, chopped	14.5 oz can diced tomatoes, no salt added	1/2 teaspoon black pepper
2 cloves garlic, minced	4 cups low-sodium vegetable broth	2 bay leaves
2 carrots, diced	1 teaspoon ground cumin	1 cup chopped kale or spinach
2 celery stalks, diced		
1 bell pepper, diced		

Directions:

1. In a large pot, heat olive oil and sauté onion and garlic until softened.
2. Add carrots, celery, and bell pepper, cooking until slightly tender.
3. Stir in lentils, diced tomatoes, vegetable broth, cumin, thyme, black pepper, and bay leaves.
4. Bring to a boil, then reduce heat to simmer, covered, for 35 minutes.
5. Add kale or spinach in the last 5 minutes, cooking until wilted and lentils are tender.
6. Discard bay leaves before serving.

Nutritional Information. Per serving: 250 calories, 18g protein, 45g carbohydrates, 3g fat, 15g fiber, 0mg cholesterol, 300mg sodium, 800mg potassium.

This stew is a perfect blend of nutrition and flavor, designed to cater to those managing diabetes while satisfying the palate of all family members. It's packed with fiber and plant-based protein, contributing to a feeling of fullness and stabilizing blood sugar levels. Low in fat and rich in vitamins and minerals, it supports overall health, making it an ideal choice for a hearty, nutritious meal.

FISHERMAN'S STEW WITH COD AND VEGETABLES

Yield: 4 servings | Prep time: 15 minutes | Cook time: 30 minutes

Ingredients:

1 pound cod fillets, cut into 1-inch pieces	2 stalks celery, diced	1 teaspoon dried thyme
2 tablespoons olive oil	1 bell pepper, any color, diced	1/2 teaspoon black pepper
1 large onion, chopped	1 can (14.5 ounces) diced tomatoes, no salt added	1/2 teaspoon paprika
2 cloves garlic, minced	4 cups low-sodium vegetable broth	1 bay leaf
2 large carrots, diced		2 tablespoons fresh parsley, chopped (for garnish)

Directions:

1. Heat olive oil in a large pot over medium heat. Sauté onion and garlic until softened, about 5 minutes.

2. Add carrots, celery, bell pepper, diced tomatoes, vegetable broth, thyme, black pepper, paprika, and bay leaf. Bring to a simmer and cook for 20 minutes.

3. Add the cod pieces to the pot and simmer for an additional 10 minutes, or until the fish is cooked through and flakes easily.

4. Garnish with fresh parsley before serving. Remove bay leaf.

Nutritional Information. Per serving: 220 calories, 23g protein, 18g carbohydrates, 7g fat, 4g fiber, 40mg cholesterol, 300mg sodium, 700mg potassium.

This Fisherman's Stew with Cod and Vegetables is an excellent meal for those managing diabetes, offering a high-protein, low-fat, and nutrient-rich option. The stew is packed with vegetables and lean protein from cod, making it heart-healthy and diabetes-friendly.

SPICY BLACK BEAN AND VEGETABLE STEW

Yield: 4 servings | Prep time: 15 minutes | Cook time: 25 minutes

Ingredients:

2 cans (15 ounces each) black beans, no salt added, rinsed and drained	2 carrots, diced	1 teaspoon chili powder
	2 stalks celery, diced	1/2 teaspoon smoked paprika
	1 can (14.5 ounces) diced tomatoes, with juice	
2 tablespoons olive oil		1/4 teaspoon cayenne pepper
1 large onion, diced	2 cups low-sodium vegetable broth	Salt and black pepper to taste
2 cloves garlic, minced		Fresh cilantro, chopped (for garnish)
1 bell pepper, diced	1 teaspoon ground cumin	

Directions:

1. Heat olive oil in a large pot over medium heat. Add onion and garlic, cook until soft, about 5 minutes.

2. Add bell pepper, carrots, and celery to the pot; cook for another 5 minutes.

3. Stir in black beans, diced tomatoes with juice, vegetable broth, cumin, chili powder, smoked paprika, cayenne pepper, salt, and black pepper. Bring to a boil, then reduce heat and simmer for 15 minutes.

4. Garnish with fresh cilantro before serving.

Nutritional Information. Per serving: 260 calories, 14g protein, 45g carbohydrates, 5g fat, 15g fiber, 0mg cholesterol, 300mg sodium, 900mg potassium.

This Spicy Black Bean and Vegetable Stew is a hearty, flavorful option for those managing diabetes. Packed with fiber-rich black beans and a variety of vegetables, it offers a balance of complex carbohydrates and protein, promoting stable blood sugar levels. The spices add a warming, satisfying dimension without the need for added sugars or unhealthy fats, making it an ideal meal for health-conscious individuals.

MOROCCAN CHICKPEA STEW

Yield: 4 servings | Prep time: 10 minutes | Cook time: 30 minutes

Ingredients:

2 tablespoons olive oil	1 can (14.5 ounces) diced tomatoes, no salt added	1/2 teaspoon ground turmeric
1 large onion, chopped	4 cups low-sodium vegetable broth	1/4 teaspoon cayenne pepper (adjust to taste)
2 cloves garlic, minced	1 teaspoon ground cumin	Salt and black pepper to taste
2 carrots, diced	1 teaspoon smoked paprika	Fresh cilantro, chopped (for garnish)
1 bell pepper, diced	1/2 teaspoon ground cinnamon	
2 cans (15 ounces each) chickpeas, drained and rinsed		

Directions:

1. In a large pot, heat olive oil over medium heat. Add onion and garlic, sauté until translucent, about 5 minutes.

2. Add carrots and bell pepper, cooking until slightly softened, about 5 minutes.

3. Stir in chickpeas, diced tomatoes with their juice, vegetable broth, cumin, paprika, cinnamon, turmeric, cayenne, salt, and black pepper. Bring to a boil, then reduce heat and simmer for 20 minutes.

4. Serve garnished with fresh cilantro.

Nutritional Information. Per serving: 290 calories, 12g protein, 49g carbohydrates, 7g fat, 13g fiber, 0mg cholesterol, 300mg sodium, 800mg potassium.

This Moroccan Chickpea Stew is a flavorful, nutritious meal suitable for those managing diabetes. Loaded with fiber from chickpeas and a variety of vegetables, it supports stable blood sugar levels and digestive health. The blend of spices not only adds a depth of flavor but also provides anti-inflammatory benefits, making this stew a deliciously healthy choice.

CHICKEN AND VEGETABLE SOUP

Yield: 4 servings | Prep time: 15 minutes | Cook time: 30 minutes

Ingredients:

1 pound boneless, skinless chicken breasts, diced	2 cloves garlic, minced	1 teaspoon dried oregano
2 tablespoons olive oil	4 cups low-sodium chicken broth	1/2 teaspoon dried basil
1 onion, chopped	1 can (14.5 ounces) diced tomatoes, no salt added, with juice	1/2 teaspoon salt (optional)
2 carrots, diced		1/2 teaspoon black pepper
2 celery stalks, diced		1 cup chopped spinach

Directions:

1. In a large pot, heat olive oil over medium heat. Add chicken and cook until browned.

2. Add onion, carrots, celery, and garlic, sautéing until the vegetables are softened.

3. Pour in chicken broth and diced tomatoes with their juice. Season with oregano, basil, salt (if using), and pepper. Bring to a boil.

4. Reduce heat to simmer, cover, and cook for 20 minutes. Stir in spinach and cook until wilted about 2 minutes.

Nutritional Information. Per serving: 230 calories, 28g protein, 15g carbohydrates, 7g fat, 4g fiber, 65mg cholesterol, 300mg sodium, 600mg potassium.

This Chicken and Vegetable Soup is a light yet nourishing meal, perfect for those managing diabetes. It combines lean protein, fiber-rich vegetables, and healthful herbs in a flavorful broth, offering a well-balanced dish that supports stable blood sugar levels. The simplicity of preparation and heartiness make it an ideal choice for a comforting lunch or dinner.

SPINACH AND WHITE BEAN SOUP

Yield: 4 servings | Prep time: 10 minutes | Cook time: 20 minutes

Ingredients:

2 tablespoons olive oil	4 cups low-sodium vegetable broth	1/2 teaspoon black pepper
1 large onion, finely chopped	2 cans (15 ounces each) white beans, rinsed and drained	1/4 teaspoon salt (optional)
2 cloves garlic, minced		4 cups fresh spinach leaves
1 teaspoon dried thyme		1 teaspoon lemon zest
		Juice of 1/2 lemon

Directions:

1. In a large pot, heat olive oil over medium heat. Sauté onion and garlic until translucent, about 5 minutes.

2. Stir in vegetable broth, white beans, thyme, black pepper, and salt. Bring to a simmer and cook for 15 minutes to blend the flavors.

3. Add spinach, lemon zest, and lemon juice. Cook until the spinach is just wilted, about 2 minutes, adjusting seasoning if necessary.

Nutritional Information. Per serving: 250 calories, 15g protein, 37g carbohydrates, 5g fat, 12g fiber, 0mg cholesterol, 300mg sodium, 1000mg potassium.

This Spinach and White Bean Soup, enriched with lemon for a fresh twist, offers a nourishing meal ideal for those managing diabetes. Its high fiber content aids in blood sugar regulation, while the protein supports muscle health. The soup's aromatic base of sautéed onion and garlic, combined with the earthiness of thyme, provides a comforting depth of flavor.

MINESTRONE SOUP WITH WHOLE WHEAT PASTA

Yield: 4 servings | Prep time: 15 minutes | Cook time: 30 minutes

Ingredients:

2 tablespoons olive oil	1 can (14.5 ounces) diced tomatoes, no salt added	1/2 teaspoon black pepper
1 onion, chopped	4 cups low-sodium vegetable broth	1 can (15 ounces) kidney beans, rinsed and drained
2 cloves garlic, minced	1 teaspoon dried oregano	1 cup whole wheat pasta, uncooked
2 carrots, diced	1/2 teaspoon dried basil	2 cups fresh spinach leaves
2 stalks celery, diced	1/2 teaspoon salt (optional)	
1 zucchini, diced		
1 cup water		

Directions:

1. In a large pot, heat olive oil over medium heat. Add onion, garlic, carrots, and celery; cook until vegetables are softened, about 5 minutes.

2. Stir in zucchini, diced tomatoes with their juice, vegetable broth, water, oregano, basil, salt, and pepper. Bring to a boil, then reduce heat and simmer for 15 minutes.

3. Add kidney beans and whole wheat pasta; cook until pasta is al dente, about 10 minutes. Stir in spinach and cook until wilted about 2 minutes.

Nutritional Information. Per serving: 320 calories, 14g protein, 54g carbohydrates, 7g fat, 12g fiber, 0mg cholesterol, 300mg sodium, 800mg potassium.

This Minestrone Soup with Whole Wheat Pasta is a hearty, comforting dish perfect for individuals managing diabetes. It's packed with vegetables, fiber-rich beans, and whole grains, making it a balanced meal that supports stable blood sugar levels. The whole wheat pasta adds a nutty flavor and satisfying texture, while the variety of vegetables ensures a nutrient-rich profile.

MUSHROOM AND WILD RICE SOUP

Yield: 4 servings | Prep time: 15 minutes | Cook time: 50 minutes

Ingredients:

1 tablespoon olive oil	1 cup wild rice, rinsed	1/4 teaspoon salt (optional)
1 large onion, chopped	5 cups low-sodium vegetable broth	1 cup unsweetened almond milk
2 cloves garlic, minced	1 teaspoon dried thyme	1/4 cup chopped fresh parsley
3 cups mixed mushrooms, chopped (shiitake, cremini, portobello)	1/2 teaspoon ground black pepper	

Directions:

1. Heat olive oil in a large pot over medium heat. Sauté onion and garlic until translucent, about 5 minutes.

2. Add mushrooms and cook until they're softened and slightly browned, about 10 minutes.

3. Stir in wild rice, vegetable broth, thyme, pepper, and salt. Bring to a boil, then reduce heat and simmer, covered, until rice is tender, about 35 minutes.

4. Once the rice is cooked, stir in almond milk and warm through without boiling, about 5 minutes. Serve garnished with parsley.

Nutritional Information. Per serving: 220 calories, 9g protein, 40g carbohydrates, 5g fat, 6g fiber, 0mg cholesterol, 200mg sodium, 300mg potassium.

This Mushroom and Wild Rice Soup offers a hearty, flavorful, and nutritious option for individuals managing diabetes. With a focus on whole grains, vegetables, and a plant-based source of creaminess, it's designed to provide balanced nutrition. The soup is low in sodium and fat, and high in fiber and protein, ensuring a satisfying meal that supports blood sugar control and overall health.

10. SNACKS AND APPETIZERS

AVOCADO DEVILED EGGS FOR DIABETICS

Yield: 6 servings | Prep time: 20 minutes | Cook time: 10 minutes

Ingredients:

6 large eggs 1 ripe avocado, peeled and pitted 1 teaspoon Dijon mustard	2 tablespoons Greek yogurt, plain 1 tablespoon lime juice Salt and pepper to taste	Paprika for garnish Fresh cilantro or parsley, chopped for garnish (optional)

Directions:

1. Place eggs in a large saucepan and cover with cold water. Bring to a boil, cover, and remove from heat. Let stand for 12 minutes. Transfer eggs to an ice-water bath to cool.

2. Peel the eggs and slice them in half lengthwise. Remove the yolks and place them in a bowl. Add the avocado, Greek yogurt, Dijon mustard, and lime juice. Mash the mixture until smooth. Season with salt and pepper to taste.

3. Spoon or pipe the avocado mixture back into the egg whites. Sprinkle with paprika and garnish with chopped cilantro or parsley if desired.

4. Chill in the refrigerator until ready to serve.

Nutritional Information. Per serving: 130 calories, 7g protein, 4g carbohydrates, 10g fat, 2g fiber, 186mg cholesterol, 125mg sodium, 230mg potassium.

This recipe provides a diabetic-friendly balance of proteins, healthy fats, and low carbohydrates, perfect for managing blood sugar levels while enjoying a flavorful snack.

VEGGIE STICKS WITH HUMMUS FOR DIABETICS

Yield: 4 servings | Prep time: 15 minutes | Cook time: 0 minutes

Ingredients:

1 cup homemade or store-bought hummus 2 large carrots, peeled and cut into sticks	1 cucumber, cut into sticks 1 bell pepper (any color), seeded and cut into sticks A pinch of smoked paprika	1 small bunch of celery, cut into sticks A drizzle of olive oil (for garnish, optional)

Directions:

1. Wash, peel (where necessary), and cut the vegetables into stick shapes. Arrange them attractively on a plate or in a serving dish.

2. Scoop the hummus into a small bowl. For a touch of flair, sprinkle paprika over the hummus and/or drizzle with olive oil. Place the bowl in the center of the serving dish, surrounded by the colorful vegetable sticks.

3. This dish can be served immediately or covered and stored in the refrigerator until needed. It's best enjoyed fresh but can be prepared a few hours ahead of time.

4. Enjoy this healthy, diabetic-friendly snack that's perfect for any time of day. It offers a delightful crunch and a creamy dip that's both nutritious and satisfying.

Nutritional Information. Per serving: 180 calories, 8g protein, 20g carbohydrates, 8g fat, 6g fiber, 0mg cholesterol, 300mg sodium, 400mg potassium.

This enhanced recipe not only provides a nutritious snack option for diabetics but also adds a gourmet touch with the garnish options, making healthy eating both delicious and visually appealing.

SMOKED SALMON CUCUMBER BITES FOR DIABETICS

Yield: 4 servings | Prep time: 20 minutes | Cook time: 0 minutes

Ingredients:

1 large English cucumber, sliced into 24 rounds 8 ounces smoked salmon, cut into bite-sized pieces	1/2 cup cream cheese, softened 1 tablespoon fresh dill, chopped, plus extra for garnish	1 tablespoon lemon juice 1/4 teaspoon black pepper 24 small capers (optional for garnish)

Directions:

1. In a small bowl, mix the cream cheese, dill, lemon juice, and black pepper until well combined. If the mixture is too thick, a little more lemon juice can be added to achieve the desired consistency.

2. Arrange the cucumber slices on a serving platter. Using a small spoon or a piping bag, dollop a small amount of the cream cheese mixture onto each cucumber slice.

3. Top each cream cheese dollop with a piece of smoked salmon. If desired, garnish each bite with a caper and a sprinkle of fresh dill.

4. Chill in the refrigerator for about 10 minutes before serving to allow the flavors to meld together nicely.

Nutritional Information. Per serving: 150 calories, 12g protein, 4g carbohydrates, 10g fat, 1g fiber, 30mg cholesterol, 670mg sodium, 200mg potassium.

This diabetic-friendly recipe combines the rich flavors of smoked salmon with the crisp freshness of cucumber, creating a delicious and nutritious appetizer that's low in carbohydrates and high in protein.

CAPRESE SKEWERS WITH CHERRY TOMATOES AND MOZZARELLA BALLS FOR DIABETICS

Yield: 4 servings | Prep time: 15 minutes | Cook time: 0 minutes

Ingredients:

24 cherry tomatoes	24 fresh basil leaves	1 tablespoon balsamic vinegar
12 small fresh mozzarella balls, halved	2 tablespoons extra-virgin olive oil	Salt and pepper to taste
		12 wooden skewers

Directions:

1. Thread a cherry tomato, a basil leaf, and a half mozzarella ball onto a skewer. Repeat the process so that each skewer has two sets of tomato, basil, and mozzarella.

2. In a small bowl, whisk together the olive oil and balsamic vinegar. Drizzle this mixture over the assembled skewers, ensuring each skewer gets an even coating.

3. Season the skewers with a sprinkle of salt and pepper to taste. Arrange them on a platter to serve.

4. Optional: For a more decorative presentation, you can drizzle additional balsamic vinegar glaze over the skewers right before serving.

Nutritional Information. Per serving: 180 calories, 12g protein, 6g carbohydrates, 13g fat, 1g fiber, 30mg cholesterol, 200mg sodium, 150mg potassium.

This simple yet elegant recipe is perfect for diabetics looking for a nutritious, low-carbohydrate option that doesn't compromise on flavor. The fresh ingredients combined with the rich balsamic and olive oil dressing make it a delightful choice for any occasion.

TUNA SALAD LETTUCE WRAPS FOR DIABETICS

Yield: 4 servings | Prep time: 15 minutes | Cook time: 0 minutes

Ingredients:

2 cans (5 ounces each) of tuna in water, drained 1/4 cup mayonnaise, low-fat 1 celery stalk, finely chopped 1 teaspoon Dijon mustard	2 tablespoons red onion, finely chopped 1 tablespoon fresh lemon juice Salt and pepper to taste	8 large lettuce leaves (e.g., romaine, butter, or iceberg) Optional garnishes: sliced avocado, diced tomatoes, or cucumber

Directions:

1. In a medium bowl, combine the drained tuna, low-fat mayonnaise, chopped celery, red onion, lemon juice, and Dijon mustard. Mix well until all ingredients are evenly incorporated. Season with salt and pepper to taste.

2. Lay out the lettuce leaves and spoon an equal amount of the tuna mixture into the center of each leaf.

3. If using, top the tuna mixture with your choice of garnishes, such as sliced avocado, diced tomatoes, or cucumber for added flavor and crunch.

4. Carefully fold the lettuce over the filling to create wraps. Serve immediately for the best texture and freshness.

Nutritional Information. Per serving: 140 calories, 20g protein, 3g carbohydrates, 5g fat, 1g fiber, 30mg cholesterol, 290mg sodium, 200mg potassium.

This diabetic-friendly recipe offers a nutritious, low-carbohydrate option that is high in protein and flavor, making it an ideal choice for a healthy lunch or light dinner.

SPICY EDAMAME FOR DIABETICS

Yield: 4 servings | Prep time: 5 minutes | Cook time: 10 minutes

Ingredients:

1 pound frozen edamame in the pod 1 tablespoon olive oil 1/2 teaspoon sea salt	1 teaspoon chili flakes (adjust to taste) 1 teaspoon garlic powder	1/4 teaspoon ground black pepper Optional: 1 teaspoon sesame seeds for garnish

Directions:

1. Boil the edamame in a pot of water for about 5 minutes, or until they are fully thawed and warm. Drain the edamame and pat them dry with paper towels.

2. Heat the olive oil in a large skillet over medium heat. Add the boiled edamame, chili flakes, garlic powder, sea salt, and ground black pepper. Stir well to ensure the edamame are evenly coated with the seasoning.

3. Cook for an additional 5 minutes, stirring occasionally, until the edamame pods are slightly charred and the flavors are well infused.

4. Remove from heat and, if desired, sprinkle sesame seeds over the top for garnish.

Nutritional Information. Per serving: 190 calories, 17g protein, 14g carbohydrates, 8g fat, 8g fiber, 0mg cholesterol, 300mg sodium, 676mg potassium.

This spicy edamame recipe offers a great mix of protein, fiber, and healthy fats, making it an ideal snack or appetizer for diabetics. The kick of heat from the chili flakes adds a delicious depth of flavor without adding extra sugar or calories.

HERB-ROASTED CHICKPEAS FOR DIABETICS

Yield: 4 servings | Preparation time: 10 minutes | Cooking time: 40 minutes

Ingredients:

2 cans (15 ounces each) chickpeas 2 tablespoons olive oil	1/2 teaspoon sea salt 1/4 teaspoon black pepper	1 teaspoon dried rosemary 1 teaspoon dried thyme 1/2 teaspoon garlic powder

Directions:

1. Preheat the oven to 400 degrees Fahrenheit. Drain and rinse the chickpeas, then pat them dry. Spread the chickpeas on a baking sheet and bake for 20 minutes.

2. In a small bowl, combine the olive oil, sea salt, black pepper, dried rosemary, dried thyme, and garlic powder. Remove the chickpeas from the oven, toss them with the olive oil mixture to coat evenly, then return them to the oven. Bake for another 20 minutes, or until they are golden and crispy.

3. Allow the chickpeas to cool before serving. They can be enjoyed as a nutritious and tasty snack.

Nutritional Information. Per serving: 210 calories, 10 grams protein, 30 grams carbohydrates, 7 grams fat, 8 grams fiber, 0 milligrams cholesterol, 300 milligrams sodium, 400 milligrams potassium.

This diabetic-friendly recipe features chickpeas roasted with a blend of herbs and spices, offering a savory snack that's high in protein and fiber. The aromatic herbs not only add flavor but also make these chickpeas a delightful, crunchy treat that's perfect for managing blood sugar levels.

11. PIZZAS AND SANDWICHES

PORTOBELLO MUSHROOM CAP PIZZA WITH SPINACH AND FETA

Yield: 4 servings | Prep time: 15 minutes | Cook time: 20 minutes

Ingredients:

4 large Portobello mushroom caps, stems and gills removed	1 cup fresh spinach, chopped	1/2 cup cherry tomatoes, halved
	1/2 cup pizza sauce, low-sodium	1/4 cup red onions, thinly sliced
		Salt and pepper to taste
1 tablespoon olive oil	1 cup crumbled feta cheese	1 teaspoon dried oregano

Directions:

1. Preheat the oven to 375 degrees Fahrenheit. Place the Portobello mushroom caps on a baking sheet, brush each cap with olive oil, and season with salt and pepper. Bake for about 10 minutes, or until the mushrooms start to release their moisture.

2. In a skillet over medium heat, sauté the spinach and red onions until the spinach is wilted and the onions are soft about 3-5 minutes.

3. Remove the mushroom caps from the oven. Spread pizza sauce evenly over each cap, then top with the sautéed spinach and onions, cherry tomatoes, and crumbled feta cheese. Sprinkle oregano over the toppings.

4. Return the mushroom caps to the oven and bake for an additional 10 minutes, or until the cheese is melted and the mushrooms are tender.

Nutritional Information. Per serving: 180 calories, 9g protein, 10g carbohydrates, 12g fat, 3g fiber, 25mg cholesterol, 400mg sodium, 500mg potassium.

This Portobello Mushroom Cap Pizza is a delightful, low-carb alternative to traditional pizza, making it perfect for diabetics. The combination of fresh spinach, tangy feta, and robust Portobello caps creates a nutritious and satisfying meal.

WHOLE WHEAT VEGGIE PIZZA WITH CAULIFLOWER CRUST

Yield: 4 servings | Prep time: 25 minutes | Cook time: 30 minutes

Ingredients:

| For the Cauliflower Crust:
1 medium head cauliflower, riced (about 2 cups)
1 egg, beaten
1/2 cup shredded mozzarella cheese
1/4 cup whole wheat flour | 1/2 teaspoon garlic powder
1 teaspoon Italian seasoning
Salt and pepper to taste
For the Toppings:
1/2 cup pizza sauce, low-sodium
1 cup shredded mozzarella cheese | 1/2 bell pepper, sliced
1/2 small red onion, sliced
1/2 cup cherry tomatoes, halved
1/4 cup black olives, sliced
1/2 cup baby spinach leaves
1 teaspoon olive oil
Red pepper flakes |

Directions:

1. Preheat your oven to 400 degrees Fahrenheit. Line a baking sheet with parchment paper.

2. For the crust, microwave the riced cauliflower in a bowl for 5 minutes, let it cool, then squeeze out excess moisture with a towel. Mix cauliflower with egg, mozzarella, whole wheat flour, Italian seasoning, garlic powder, salt, and pepper.

3. Spread the cauliflower mixture onto the lined baking sheet, shaping it into a pizza crust about 1/4 inch thick. Bake for 20 minutes, or until golden.

4. Remove the crust from the oven, spread pizza sauce over it, then top with mozzarella, bell pepper, red onion, cherry tomatoes, olives, and spinach. Drizzle with olive oil.

5. Bake for an additional 10 minutes, or until the cheese is bubbly and the veggies are tender. Garnish with red pepper flakes if desired.

Nutritional Information. Per serving: 230 calories, 15 grams protein, 20 grams carbohydrates, 10 grams fat, 5 grams fiber, 45 milligrams cholesterol, 320 milligrams sodium, 400 milligrams potassium.

This Whole Wheat Veggie Pizza on a Cauliflower Crust is a healthier twist on traditional pizza, perfect for diabetics looking for a low-carb option. It combines the nutritional benefits of whole grains, vegetables, and a creative cauliflower crust for a delicious, guilt-free meal.

BBQ CHICKEN PITA PIZZA WITH RED ONION AND BELL PEPPER

Yield: 4 servings | Prep time: 15 minutes | Cook time: 10 minutes

Ingredients

4 whole wheat pita breads 1 cup cooked chicken breast, shredded 1/2 cup low-sugar BBQ sauce	1 red onion, thinly sliced 1 bell pepper, thinly sliced 1 cup shredded low-fat mozzarella cheese	2 tablespoons fresh cilantro, chopped (optional for garnish) Salt and pepper to taste

Directions

1. Preheat the oven to 425°F. Place the pita breads on a large baking sheet.

2. Spread each pita evenly with BBQ sauce. Top with shredded chicken, sliced red onion, and bell pepper. Sprinkle with shredded mozzarella cheese and season with a pinch of salt and pepper.

3. Bake in the preheated oven for 8-10 minutes, or until the cheese is melted and bubbly and the edges of the pita are crispy.

4. Remove from the oven, garnish with fresh cilantro if desired, and serve immediately.

Nutritional Information. Per serving: 350 calories, 25g protein, 45g carbohydrates, 9g fat, 6g fiber, 50mg cholesterol, 600mg sodium, 300mg potassium.

This BBQ Chicken Pita Pizza is a delicious, diabetes-friendly meal that offers a balance of lean protein, complex carbohydrates, and low-fat dairy, making it an excellent choice for managing blood sugar levels. The use of whole wheat pita and low-sugar BBQ sauce helps keep the glycemic index lower, while still delivering a satisfying and flavorful pizza experience.

TURKEY AND AVOCADO SANDWICH ON WHOLE GRAIN BREAD

Yield: 6 servings | Prep time: 10 minutes | Cook time: 0 minutes

Ingredients

12 slices whole grain bread 1 lb sliced turkey breast, low sodium 2 tomatoes, sliced	2 ripe avocados, peeled, pitted, and sliced 1/2 red onion, thinly sliced 1 tablespoon mustard	6 lettuce leaves, washed and dried 3 tablespoons low-fat mayonnaise Salt and pepper to taste

Directions

1. Spread each slice of bread lightly with low-fat mayonnaise and mustard.

2. On six slices of bread, layer the sliced turkey breast, avocado slices, red onion, tomato slices, and lettuce. Season with a little salt and pepper to taste.

3. Top with the remaining slices of bread. Press down gently, then cut each sandwich in half diagonally.

4. Serve immediately or wrap in parchment paper for a grab-and-go lunch option.

Nutritional Information. Per serving: 380 calories, 28g protein, 40g carbohydrates, 12g fat, 8g fiber, 45mg cholesterol, 580mg sodium, 700mg potassium.

This Turkey and Avocado Sandwich on Whole Grain Bread offers a hearty, nutritious option that is perfect for diabetics, focusing on high fiber, healthy fats, and lean protein to help maintain blood sugar levels. The use of whole-grain bread and fresh vegetables adds essential nutrients and fiber, making it a balanced meal for any time of the day.

EGGPLANT PARMESAN SANDWICH ON WHOLE WHEAT CIABATTA

Yield: 4 servings | Prep time: 20 minutes | Cook time: 30 minutes

Ingredients

1 large eggplant, sliced into 1/2-inch rounds 1/4 cup olive oil 4 whole wheat ciabatta rolls, split in half	Salt and pepper to taste 1 cup marinara sauce, low-sodium 1 cup shredded part-skim mozzarella cheese	1/4 cup grated Parmesan cheese 1 teaspoon dried oregano 1 teaspoon dried basil Fresh basil leaves for garnish

Directions

1. Preheat the oven to 400°F. Brush both sides of the eggplant slices with olive oil and season with salt and pepper. Arrange on a baking sheet and bake for 25 minutes, flipping halfway through, until tender and golden.

2. Spread a tablespoon of marinara sauce on each ciabatta half. Layer the baked eggplant slices on the bottom halves of the ciabatta rolls. Top with mozzarella and Parmesan cheeses, oregano, and dried basil.

3. Place the open sandwiches back into the oven and bake for an additional 5 minutes, or until the cheese is melted and bubbly.

4. Close the sandwiches with the top halves of the ciabatta, garnish with fresh basil if desired, and serve immediately.

Nutritional Information. Per serving: 410 calories, 18g protein, 45g carbohydrates, 20g fat, 9g fiber, 30mg cholesterol, 610mg sodium, 700mg potassium.

This Eggplant Parmesan Sandwich on Whole Wheat Ciabatta offers a delicious and diabetic-friendly twist on a classic Italian favorite, incorporating whole grains and vegetables for a balanced meal. The combination of baked eggplant, marinara sauce, and melted cheese on whole wheat ciabatta provides a satisfying yet healthy option suitable for managing blood sugar levels.

OPEN-FACED TUNA MELT ON WHOLE GRAIN ENGLISH MUFFIN

Yield: 4 servings | Prep time: 10 minutes | Cook time: 5 minutes

Ingredients

4 whole grain English muffins, split and toasted	1/4 cup low-fat mayonnaise	2 tablespoons finely chopped red onion
2 cans (6 ounces each) of tuna in water, drained	1/4 cup finely chopped celery	Salt and pepper to taste
1 tablespoon lemon juice	8 tomato slices	1 cup shredded low-fat cheddar cheese

Directions

1. In a medium bowl, mix the drained tuna, low-fat mayonnaise, chopped celery, chopped red onion, and lemon juice. Season with salt and pepper to taste.

2. Place the toasted English muffin halves on a baking sheet. Divide the tuna mixture evenly among the muffin halves, spreading it to cover.

3. Top each with two tomato slices and sprinkle with shredded low-fat cheddar cheese.

4. Broil in the oven for about 3-5 minutes, or until the cheese is melted and bubbly. Watch carefully to avoid burning.

5. Serve immediately while warm.

Nutritional Information. Per serving: 330 calories, 28g protein, 38g carbohydrates, 9g fat, 5g fiber, 35mg cholesterol, 580mg sodium, 400mg potassium.

This Open-Faced Tuna Melt on Whole Grain English Muffin is a hearty, nutritious option for diabetics, focusing on high protein, fiber-rich whole grains, and low-fat ingredients to help manage blood sugar levels. The use of whole-grain English muffins instead of traditional bread helps increase the fiber content, which is beneficial for maintaining a healthy digestive system and supporting blood sugar control.

CAPRESE FLATBREAD WITH TOMATO, BASIL, AND FRESH MOZZARELLA

Yield: 4 servings | Prep time: 10 minutes | Cook time: 10 minutes

Ingredients

1 large flatbread or naan	8 ounces fresh mozzarella cheese, sliced	Salt and pepper to taste
2 tablespoons olive oil		Balsamic glaze for drizzling
2 large tomatoes, thinly sliced	1/4 cup fresh basil leaves	(optional)

Directions

1. Preheat your oven to 400°F. Place the flatbread on a baking sheet and brush it evenly with olive oil.

2. Arrange the tomato slices evenly over the flatbread, followed by the mozzarella slices. Season with salt and pepper.

3. Bake in the preheated oven for about 10 minutes, or until the cheese is melted and bubbly, and the edges of the flatbread are crispy and golden.

4. Remove from the oven and immediately top with fresh basil leaves. Drizzle with balsamic glaze if desired.

5. Cut into pieces and serve warm.

Nutritional Information. Per serving: 350 calories, 18g protein, 25g carbohydrates, 20g fat, 2g fiber, 45mg cholesterol, 480mg sodium, 200mg potassium.

This Caprese Flatbread combines the classic flavors of a traditional Caprese salad with the hearty, satisfying base of a crispy flatbread. The fresh tomatoes, creamy mozzarella, and aromatic basil create a simple yet elegant dish, perfect for a light lunch, appetizer, or part of a shared meal. The optional drizzle of balsamic glaze adds a sweet and tangy finish that elevates the flavors.

TURKEY AND CRANBERRY PANINI ON WHOLE GRAIN BREAD

Yield: 2 servings | Prep time: 10 minutes | Cook time: 10 minutes

Ingredients:

4 slices whole grain bread 6 ounces sliced turkey breast	1/4 cup cranberry sauce 2 tablespoons Dijon mustard	2 slices Swiss cheese 2 teaspoons olive oil or cooking spray

Directions:

1. Preheat a panini press or grill pan over medium heat.
2. Spread Dijon mustard on two slices of bread. Top each with turkey slices, cranberry sauce, and a slice of Swiss cheese. Place the remaining bread slices on top.
3. Brush the outsides of the sandwiches lightly with olive oil or coat with cooking spray.
4. Place the sandwiches on the panini press or grill pan and cook until the bread is golden brown and crispy, and the cheese is melted, about 4-5 minutes.
5. Carefully remove the sandwiches from the press or pan, slice in half, and serve hot.

Nutritional Information. Per serving: 384 calories, 26g protein, 39g carbohydrates, 14g fat, 5g fiber, 50mg cholesterol, 527mg sodium, 253mg potassium.

This Turkey and Cranberry Panini on Whole Grain Bread is a delightful combination of savory turkey, tangy cranberry sauce, and melty Swiss cheese, all nestled between hearty whole grain bread. It's a satisfying and balanced meal that's perfect for a quick lunch or dinner option.

12. DAIRY DISHES

LOW-FAT COTTAGE CHEESE AND TOMATO SALAD

Yield: 4 servings | Prep time: 10 minutes | Cook time: 0 minutes

Ingredients

2 cups low-fat cottage cheese 4 large tomatoes, diced 1/2 cup cucumber, diced	1/4 cup red onion, finely chopped 2 tablespoons fresh basil, chopped	1 tablespoon olive oil 1 tablespoon balsamic vinegar Salt and pepper to taste

Directions

1. In a large bowl, combine the low-fat cottage cheese, diced tomatoes, cucumber, and red onion.

2. Add the chopped fresh basil to the mixture for a burst of flavor.

3. Drizzle olive oil and balsamic vinegar over the salad. Season with salt and pepper to taste. Gently toss to combine all the ingredients evenly.

4. Chill in the refrigerator for about 30 minutes before serving to allow the flavors to meld together.

5. Serve chilled, garnished with additional basil if desired.

Nutritional Information. Per serving: 150 calories, 14g protein, 10g carbohydrates, 5g fat, 2g fiber, 5mg cholesterol, 400mg sodium, 350mg potassium.

This Low-Fat Cottage Cheese and Tomato Salad is a refreshing, nutritious option perfect for a light lunch or as a healthy side dish. Featuring a combination of creamy low-fat cottage cheese, crisp vegetables, and a tangy dressing, it's a delicious way to enjoy fresh produce while keeping your meal light and low in calories.

GREEK YOGURT CHICKEN SALAD WITH APPLES AND ALMONDS

Yield: 4 servings | Prep time: 20 minutes | Cook time: 0 minutes

Ingredients:

2 cups cooked chicken, shredded	1/2 cup celery, chopped	2 tablespoons lemon juice
1 cup Greek yogurt	1/2 cup almonds, sliced	Salt and pepper to taste
1 medium apple, diced	1/4 cup red onion, finely chopped	Lettuce leaves, for serving (optional)

Directions:

1. In a large mixing bowl, combine the shredded chicken, Greek yogurt, diced apple, chopped celery, sliced almonds, and finely chopped red onion.

2. Add the lemon juice to the mixture and season with salt and pepper. Stir well to ensure all ingredients are evenly coated with the Greek yogurt.

3. Taste and adjust the seasoning as necessary. If the salad seems a little dry, you can add a bit more Greek yogurt to reach the desired consistency.

4. Serve the chicken salad on a bed of lettuce leaves or as a filling for sandwiches or wraps.

Nutritional Information. Per serving: calories: 290, protein: 25g, carbohydrates: 14g, fat: 16g, fiber: 3g, cholesterol: 55mg, sodium: 190mg, potassium: 300mg.

This recipe combines the lean protein from the chicken, the creaminess of the Greek yogurt, and the crunch from the apples and almonds for a refreshing and nutritious meal. Perfect for a light lunch or a healthy snack!

COTTAGE CHEESE PANCAKES WITH FRESH FRUIT

Yield: 4 servings | Prep time: 10 minutes | Cook time: 15 minutes

Ingredients:

1 cup cottage cheese	1 tablespoon sugar	Fresh fruit (berries, sliced bananas, etc.) for serving
2 large eggs	1 teaspoon baking powder	
1/2 cup all-purpose flour	1/2 teaspoon vanilla extract	Optional: Maple syrup or honey for serving
1/4 cup milk	Butter or oil for cooking	

Directions:

1. In a large bowl, mix the cottage cheese, eggs, milk, and vanilla extract until well combined. In a separate bowl, whisk together the flour, sugar, and baking powder.

2. Gradually add the dry ingredients to the wet ingredients, stirring until just combined. Be careful not to overmix.

3. Heat a non-stick skillet or griddle over medium heat and lightly grease with butter or oil. Pour 1/4 cup of batter for each pancake onto the skillet. Cook until bubbles form on the surface, then flip and cook until golden brown on the other side, about 2 minutes per side.

4. Serve the pancakes warm, topped with fresh fruit and optional maple syrup or honey.

Nutritional Information. Per serving: calories: 220, protein: 14g, carbohydrates: 24g, fat: 8g, fiber: 1g, cholesterol: 110mg, sodium: 340mg, potassium: 200mg.

This recipe offers a high-protein, satisfying breakfast option that incorporates the creamy texture of cottage cheese with the sweetness of fresh fruit, making it a delightful start to any day.

TOFU AND VEGETABLE STIR-FRY WITH SOY MILK SAUCE

Yield: 4 servings | Prep time: 15 minutes | Cook time: 10 minutes

Ingredients:

1 block (14 oz) firm tofu, drained and cubed	1 carrot, sliced	1 tablespoon cornstarch
2 tablespoons vegetable oil	2 green onions, chopped	1 tablespoon water
1 red bell pepper, sliced	1 garlic clove, minced	1 teaspoon sesame oil
1 cup broccoli florets	1/4 cup soy sauce	Salt and pepper to taste
	1/2 cup unsweetened soy milk	Sesame seeds for garnish

Directions:

1. Heat vegetable oil in a large pan or wok over medium-high heat. Add the cubed tofu and cook until all sides are golden brown, about 5 minutes. Remove tofu from the pan and set aside.

2. In the same pan, add the red bell pepper, broccoli, and carrot. Stir-fry for about 3 minutes until the vegetables are just tender. Add the green onions and minced garlic, cooking for another minute.

3. In a small bowl, whisk together soy sauce, soy milk, cornstarch, and water until smooth. Pour this sauce into the pan with the vegetables and bring to a simmer. Return the tofu to the pan. Stir everything together and cook until the sauce thickens, about 2 minutes.

4. Drizzle with sesame oil and season with salt and pepper to taste. Garnish with sesame seeds before serving.

Nutritional Information. Per serving: calories: 220, protein: 12g, carbohydrates: 15g, fat: 13g, fiber: 3g, cholesterol: 0mg, sodium: 870mg, potassium: 300mg.

This Tofu and Vegetable Stir-Fry with Soy Milk Sauce combines the hearty textures of tofu and fresh vegetables with a creamy, savory sauce for a delicious and nutritious meal that's easy to prepare. Perfect for a quick dinner or a healthy lunch!

RICOTTA AND SPINACH STUFFED MUSHROOMS

Yield: 4 servings | Prep time: 15 minutes | Cook time: 20 minutes

Ingredients:

16 large mushrooms, stems removed	2 cups spinach, chopped	Salt and pepper to taste
	1 cup ricotta cheese	1/4 teaspoon nutmeg
1 tablespoon olive oil	1/4 cup grated Parmesan cheese	1/2 cup breadcrumbs
1 clove garlic, minced		2 tablespoons melted butter

Directions:

1. Preheat the oven to 375°F (190°C). Arrange the mushroom caps on a baking sheet, hollow side up.

2. Heat the olive oil in a pan over medium heat. Add the garlic and sauté for 1 minute. Add the spinach and cook until wilted about 3 minutes. Remove from heat and let cool slightly.

3. In a bowl, mix the spinach with ricotta, Parmesan, salt, pepper, and nutmeg. Fill each mushroom cap with the mixture.

4. Combine the breadcrumbs with melted butter, then sprinkle over the stuffed mushrooms. Bake for 20 minutes, or until the mushrooms are tender and the tops are golden brown.

Nutritional Information. Per serving: calories: 220, protein: 12g, carbohydrates: 15g, fat: 13g, fiber: 3g, cholesterol: 30mg, sodium: 370mg, potassium: 300mg.

These Ricotta and Spinach Stuffed Mushrooms are a delicious and elegant appetizer or side dish, perfect for entertaining or a cozy dinner at home. The creamy ricotta and spinach filling, paired with the earthy flavor of mushrooms, makes for a delightful combination that's sure to impress.

SKIM MILK OATMEAL WITH BERRIES

Yield: 4 servings | Prep time: 5 minutes | Cook time: 10 minutes

Ingredients:

2 cups skim milk	1/2 teaspoon vanilla extract	1/4 teaspoon salt
1 cup old-fashioned oats	1 cup mixed berries (such as blueberries, raspberries, and sliced strawberries)	Additional berries and a sprinkle of cinnamon for garnish (optional)
1 tablespoon honey or maple syrup (optional)		

Directions:

1. In a medium saucepan, bring the skim milk to a boil over medium heat. Watch carefully to prevent it from boiling over.

2. Stir in the oats, reduce the heat to low, and simmer for 5 minutes, or until the oats are tender and have absorbed most of the milk, stirring occasionally.

3. Remove from heat and stir in the honey (or maple syrup), vanilla extract, and salt. Let sit for 2 minutes to thicken.

4. Serve the oatmeal in bowls topped with mixed berries. Garnish with additional berries and a sprinkle of cinnamon if desired.

Nutritional information. Per serving: calories: 150, protein: 6g, carbohydrates: 27g, fat: 2g, fiber: 4g, cholesterol: 2mg, sodium: 160mg, potassium: 350mg.

This Skim Milk Oatmeal with Berries recipe offers a nutritious and heartwarming start to your day. Packed with the goodness of whole grains and the antioxidant power of berries, it's a deliciously healthy breakfast option that's both easy to make and satisfying.

GREEK YOGURT RANCH DIP WITH VEGGIE STICKS

Yield: 4 servings | Prep time: 10 minutes | Cook time: 0 minutes

Ingredients:

1 cup Greek yogurt	1 tablespoon fresh chives, finely chopped	Salt and pepper to taste
1 tablespoon fresh dill, finely chopped	1/2 teaspoon onion powder	Assorted vegetable sticks (carrots, bell peppers, cucumbers, and celery)
1 clove garlic, minced		

Directions:

1. In a medium bowl, combine Greek yogurt, dill, chives, minced garlic, onion powder, salt, and pepper. Stir until all ingredients are well blended.

2. Taste and adjust the seasoning as needed. For a thinner consistency, a little water or milk can be mixed in.

3. Chill the dip for at least 30 minutes before serving to allow the flavors to meld.

4. Serve with an assortment of vegetable sticks for dipping.

Nutritional information. Per serving: calories: 60, protein: 6g, carbohydrates: 4g, fat: 2g, fiber: 0.5g, cholesterol: 10mg, sodium: 45mg, potassium: 90mg.

This Greek Yogurt Ranch Dip with Veggie Sticks is a healthy and delicious snack that's perfect for parties or as a nutritious snack option. The creamy texture of Greek yogurt combined with fresh herbs makes for a flavorful alternative to traditional ranch dips, offering a great way to enjoy your favorite vegetables.

GREEK YOGURT BERRY PARFAIT WITH ALMOND GRANOLA

Yield: 4 servings | Prep time: 15 minutes | Cook time: 0 minutes

Ingredients:

2 cups Greek yogurt, for a creamy base 2 tablespoons honey or maple syrup, to enhance the flavors	1 cup almond granola, adding a delightful crunch 1 cup mixed berries (strawberries, blueberries, raspberries)	Optional garnishes: mint leaves for freshness, additional honey or maple syrup for extra sweetness

Directions:

1. Start by layering 1/4 cup of Greek yogurt in serving glasses or bowls, creating the first creamy layer.

2. Follow with a generous layer of 2 tablespoons of almond granola, introducing a crunchy texture.

3. Add a colorful layer of mixed berries on top, offering a burst of freshness.

4. Continue layering yogurt, granola, and berries until glasses are filled, ensuring to end with a top layer of juicy berries.

5. Drizzle with honey or maple syrup for added sweetness and garnish with mint leaves if using, for a refreshing finish. Enjoy immediately or chill in the refrigerator until ready to serve.

Nutritional information. Per serving: calories: 250, protein: 12g, carbohydrates: 34g, fat: 8g, fiber: 4g, cholesterol: 10mg, sodium: 65mg, potassium: 200mg.

This enhanced Greek Yogurt Berry Parfait with Almond Granola is not just a treat for the taste buds but also a visually appealing, nutritious option for breakfast or snack time. The combination of smooth Greek yogurt, crunchy almond granola, and sweet mixed berries, all beautifully layered in a glass, makes this dish a delightful way to start your day or enjoy a healthy snack.

LOW-CARB CRUSTLESS QUICHE WITH BROCCOLI AND CHEDDAR

Yield: 4 servings | Prep time: 10 minutes | Cook time: 35 minutes

Ingredients:

4 large eggs	1 cup shredded cheddar cheese	1/4 teaspoon garlic powder
1 cup heavy cream		1/4 teaspoon onion powder
2 cups broccoli florets, steamed and chopped	1/2 teaspoon salt	Non-stick cooking spray or butter for greasing
	1/4 teaspoon black pepper	

Directions:

1. Preheat the oven to 350°F (175°C). Grease a 9-inch pie dish with non-stick cooking spray or butter.

2. In a large bowl, whisk together eggs, heavy cream, salt, pepper, garlic powder, and onion powder until well combined.

3. Stir in the steamed and chopped broccoli and shredded cheddar cheese into the egg mixture. Pour the mixture into the prepared pie dish.

4. Bake in the preheated oven for 35 minutes, or until the center is set and the top is lightly golden.

5. Let the quiche cool for a few minutes before slicing and serving.

Nutritional information. Per serving: calories: 320, protein: 18g, carbohydrates: 6g, fat: 26g, fiber: 2g, cholesterol: 215mg, sodium: 470mg, potassium: 250mg.

This Low-Carb Crustless Quiche with Broccoli and Cheddar is a delicious, easy-to-make dish that's perfect for any meal of the day. Packed with protein and full of flavor, it's a healthy option for those following a low-carb lifestyle or anyone looking for a nutritious and satisfying meal.

FETA AND SPINACH EGG MUFFINS

Yield: 6 servings | Prep time: 10 minutes | Cook time: 20 minutes

Ingredients:

8 large eggs	1/2 cup feta cheese, crumbled	1/4 cup red bell pepper, finely diced
1/2 cup milk	Salt and pepper to taste	Non-stick cooking spray
1 cup fresh spinach, chopped		

Directions:

1. Preheat your oven to 350°F (175°C) and generously spray a 12-cup muffin tin with non-stick cooking spray.

2. In a large mixing bowl, whisk together eggs and milk until well combined. Season with salt and pepper.

3. Stir in the chopped spinach, crumbled feta cheese, and diced red bell pepper.

4. Divide the mixture evenly among the prepared muffin cups, filling each about two-thirds full.

5. Bake in the preheated oven for 20 minutes, or until the egg muffins are set and lightly golden on top.

Nutritional information. Per serving: calories: 150, protein: 12g, carbohydrates: 3g, fat: 10g, fiber: 0.5g, cholesterol: 215mg, sodium: 320mg, potassium: 125mg.

These Feta and Spinach Egg Muffins are a delicious, easy-to-make option for breakfast or a quick snack. Packed with protein and low in carbs, they're perfect for those on a low-carb diet or anyone looking for a healthy meal on the go. The combination of feta and spinach not only adds a wonderful flavor but also provides a good amount of nutrients, making these muffins a healthy and satisfying choice.

13. DESSERTS

BANANA NICE CREAM (FROZEN BANANA BLEND)

Yield: 4 servings | Prep time: 10 minutes (plus freezing time for bananas) | Cook time: 0 minutes

Ingredients:

4 large ripe bananas, sliced and frozen 1 teaspoon vanilla extract	1/4 cup almond milk (or any milk of choice)	Optional add-ins: chocolate chips, peanut butter, berries, or nuts

Directions:

1. Place the frozen banana slices in a food processor or high-speed blender. Add the almond milk and vanilla extract.

2. Blend on high until the mixture is smooth and creamy, stopping to scrape down the sides as necessary. If using, add your optional mix-ins and pulse a few times to incorporate.

3. Serve immediately for a soft-serve texture, or transfer to a freezer-safe container and freeze for 2-3 hours for a firmer ice cream consistency.

4. Scoop into bowls and enjoy a healthy, refreshing treat.

Nutritional information. Per serving: calories: 105, protein: 1.5g, carbohydrates: 27g, fat: 0.5g, fiber: 3g, cholesterol: 0mg, sodium: 5mg, potassium: 422mg.

Banana Nice Cream is a simple, wholesome alternative to traditional ice cream, offering the creamy texture and sweet taste of ice cream with none of the added sugar or dairy. It's a perfect dessert for those looking for a healthier option or anyone with dietary restrictions. Enjoy it plain or get creative with various mix-ins for an extra flavor boost!

BAKED APPLES STUFFED WITH CINNAMON AND WALNUTS

Yield: 4 servings | Prep time: 15 minutes | Cook time: 30 minutes

Ingredients:

4 large apples, such as Honeycrisp or Granny Smith	1/2 cup walnuts, chopped 1/4 cup brown sugar 1 teaspoon cinnamon	1/4 teaspoon nutmeg 2 tablespoons butter, melted 1/2 cup apple cider or water

Directions:

1. Preheat your oven to 375°F (190°C). Core the apples and make a wide well in the center, being careful not to cut through the bottom.

2. In a bowl, combine the chopped walnuts, brown sugar, cinnamon, and nutmeg. Stir in the melted butter until the mixture is well combined.

3. Stuff each apple with the walnut mixture, packing it tightly.

4. Place the stuffed apples in a baking dish and pour the apple cider or water into the bottom of the dish.

5. Bake in the preheated oven for 30 minutes, or until the apples are tender and the stuffing is bubbly.

Nutritional information. Per serving: calories: 260, protein: 2g, carbohydrates: 38g, fat: 12g, fiber: 5g, cholesterol: 15mg, sodium: 30mg, potassium: 240mg.

These Baked Apples Stuffed with Cinnamon and Walnuts are a warm, comforting dessert perfect for chilly evenings. The sweet blend of spices and the crunch of walnuts create a delightful contrast with the soft, baked apples. Serving these as a treat not only offers a delicious end to any meal but also fills your home with a wonderful, inviting aroma.

SUGAR-FREE PUMPKIN PIE WITH A NUT CRUST

Yield: 6 servings | Prep time: 20 minutes | Cook time: 55 minutes

Ingredients:

For the Nut Crust:	1 tablespoon erythritol (or	2 large eggs
1 1/2 cups mixed nuts (almonds, pecans, walnuts), finely ground	another sugar substitute)	1 teaspoon vanilla extract
	For the Filling:	1 teaspoon ground cinnamon
	1 (15 oz) can of pumpkin puree	1/2 teaspoon ground ginger
1/4 cup unsalted butter, melted	3/4 cup heavy cream	1/4 teaspoon ground nutmeg
1/2 teaspoon cinnamon	1/2 cup erythritol	1/4 teaspoon salt

Directions:

1. Preheat your oven to 350°F (175°C). In a bowl, mix the ground nuts, melted butter, erythritol, and cinnamon until well combined. Press the mixture into the bottom and up the sides of a 9-inch pie plate. Bake for 10 minutes, then remove from the oven and let cool.

2. For the filling, whisk together pumpkin puree, heavy cream, erythritol, eggs, vanilla extract, cinnamon, ginger, nutmeg, and salt in a large bowl until smooth. Pour the filling into the cooled nut crust.

3. Bake in the preheated oven for 45 minutes, or until the filling is set and a knife inserted near the center comes out clean. Let the pie cool completely on a wire rack.

4. Refrigerate for at least 4 hours before serving. Garnish with whipped cream if desired.

Nutritional information. Per serving: calories: 350, protein: 8g, carbohydrates: 15g, fat: 30g, fiber: 4g, cholesterol: 115mg, sodium: 150mg, potassium: 200mg.

This Sugar-Free Pumpkin Pie with a Nut Crust offers a delightful twist on the classic fall dessert, perfect for those watching their sugar intake without sacrificing flavor. The rich, creamy pumpkin filling pairs beautifully with the crunchy nut crust, making it a guilt-free indulgence for your next holiday gathering or a cozy night.

SUGAR-FREE BERRY CRISP WITH OAT TOPPING

Yield: 4 servings | Prep time: 15 minutes | Cook time: 30 minutes

Ingredients:

| For the Berry Filling:
4 cups mixed berries (such as strawberries, blueberries, raspberries, blackberries), fresh or frozen
1/4 cup erythritol (or another sugar substitute) | 1 tablespoon lemon juice
1 tablespoon arrowroot powder or cornstarch
For the Oat Topping:
1 cup rolled oats
1/2 cup almond flour
1/4 cup erythritol | 1/4 cup chopped nuts (almonds, walnuts, or pecans)
1/2 teaspoon cinnamon
1/4 cup unsalted butter, melted
Pinch of salt |

Directions:

1. Preheat the oven to 375°F (190°C). In a mixing bowl, combine the mixed berries, erythritol, lemon juice, and arrowroot powder. Stir gently until the berries are evenly coated. Transfer the berry mixture to an 8-inch square baking dish.

2. In a separate bowl, mix together the rolled oats, almond flour, chopped nuts, erythritol, cinnamon, and a pinch of salt. Pour in the melted butter and mix until the dry ingredients are moistened.

3. Sprinkle the oat mixture evenly over the berry filling in the baking dish. Bake in the preheated oven for about 30 minutes, or until the topping is golden brown and the berry filling is bubbling.

4. Let the berry crisp and cool slightly before serving. It can be enjoyed warm or at room temperature.

Nutritional information. Per serving: calories: 300, protein: 6g, carbohydrates: 34g, fat: 18g, fiber: 7g, cholesterol: 30mg, sodium: 75mg, potassium: 200mg.

This Sugar-Free Berry Crisp with Oat Topping offers a delightful and healthier alternative to traditional dessert crisps. The juicy, tangy berry filling combined with a crunchy, nutty topping makes for a satisfying treat that doesn't skimp on flavor. Perfect for those looking to reduce their sugar intake without sacrificing their sweet tooth!

ALMOND FLOUR BLUEBERRY MUFFINS

Yield: 6 servings | Prep time: 15 minutes | Cook time: 25 minutes

Ingredients:

2 cups almond flour	1 teaspoon baking powder	1/3 cup unsweetened almond milk
1/2 cup erythritol (or another granulated sugar substitute)	1/4 teaspoon salt	1 teaspoon vanilla extract
	3 large eggs	1 cup fresh blueberries
	1/4 cup coconut oil, melted	

Directions:

1. Preheat your oven to 350°F (175°C) and line a muffin tin with paper liners or grease with non-stick cooking spray.

2. In a large bowl, mix the almond flour, erythritol, baking powder, and salt.

3. In a separate bowl, whisk the eggs, almond milk melted coconut oil, and vanilla extract until well combined. Pour the wet ingredients into the dry ingredients and stir until just combined. Gently fold in the blueberries.

4. Divide the batter evenly among the prepared muffin cups, filling each about two-thirds full.

5. Bake in the preheated oven for 20-25 minutes, or until a toothpick inserted into the center of a muffin comes out clean.

Nutritional information. Per serving: calories: 320, protein: 10g, carbohydrates: 15g, fat: 27g, fiber: 4g, cholesterol: 93mg, sodium: 125mg, potassium: 100mg.

These Almond Flour Blueberry Muffins are a delicious, low-carb option for those looking for a healthier alternative to traditional muffins. Made with wholesome ingredients, these muffins are moist, fluffy, and bursting with blueberries, offering a satisfying treat without the guilt. Perfect for breakfast, a snack, or any time you need a sweet, nutritious boost!

CHIA SEED PUDDING WITH UNSWEETENED ALMOND MILK

Yield: 4 servings | Prep time: 5 minutes | Cook time: 0 minutes

(Refrigeration time: at least 2 hours or overnight)

Ingredients:

1/2 cup chia seeds 2 cups unsweetened almond milk	1 tablespoon maple syrup or honey (optional, for sweetness)	1 teaspoon vanilla extract Fresh fruits and nuts for topping (optional)

Directions:

1. In a mixing bowl, combine the chia seeds, almond milk, maple syrup (if using), and vanilla extract. Stir well until the mixture begins to thicken.

2. Cover the bowl with a lid or plastic wrap and refrigerate for at least 2 hours, or overnight, allowing the chia seeds to swell and absorb the liquid, forming a pudding-like consistency.

3. Before serving, stir the pudding again to break up any clumps. If the pudding is too thick, you can add a little more almond milk to reach your desired consistency.

4. Serve the chia pudding in individual bowls or glasses, topped with fresh fruits and nuts of your choice.

Nutritional information. Per serving: calories: 150, protein: 5g, carbohydrates: 15g, fat: 8g, fiber: 10g, cholesterol: 0mg, sodium: 90mg, potassium: 200mg.

This Chia Seed Pudding with Unsweetened Almond Milk is a simple, nutritious, and delicious recipe that serves as a perfect breakfast, snack, or dessert. It's rich in fiber, protein, and omega-3 fatty acids, making it not only a tasty choice but also a healthful one. The addition of fresh fruits and nuts not only adds to its nutritional value but also enhances its flavor and texture, making it a versatile dish that can be customized to suit your taste preferences.

LOW-CARB CHEESECAKE WITH ALMOND FLOUR CRUST

Yield: 6 servings | Prep time: 20 minutes | Cook time: 50 minutes

Ingredients:

For the Crust: 1 1/2 cups almond flour 1/4 cup unsalted butter, melted 1 teaspoon vanilla extract	1 tablespoon erythritol (or another sugar substitute) For the Filling: 16 ounces cream cheese, softened	1 cup erythritol 2 large eggs 1/4 cup sour cream 1 tablespoon lemon juice 1 teaspoon vanilla extract

Directions:

1. Preheat your oven to 350°F (175°C). For the crust, combine almond flour, melted butter, erythritol, and vanilla extract in a bowl. Mix until well combined and press the mixture into the bottom of a 9-inch springform pan. Bake for 10 minutes, then remove from oven and let cool.

2. For the filling, beat the cream cheese and erythritol together in a large bowl until smooth. Add eggs one at a time, beating well after each addition. Mix in sour cream, lemon juice, and vanilla extract until smooth.

3. Pour the filling over the cooled crust and smooth the top with a spatula. Bake in the preheated oven for 40 minutes, or until the center is just set and the top appears slightly dry.

4. Turn off the oven and leave the cheesecake inside with the door closed for another hour. Afterward, remove from the oven, cool to room temperature, then refrigerate until fully chilled, at least 4 hours or overnight.

5. Serve chilled, optionally garnished with fresh berries or a sugar-free sauce.

Nutritional information. Per serving: calories: 420, protein: 12g, carbohydrates: 9g, fat: 38g, fiber: 2g, cholesterol: 150mg, sodium: 320mg, potassium: 180mg.

This Low-Carb Cheesecake with Almond Flour Crust is a delicious dessert that fits perfectly into a low-carb or keto lifestyle. The creamy filling and nutty crust offer the classic cheesecake experience without the guilt. It's an excellent choice for special occasions or whenever you crave something sweet and satisfying.

DARK CHOCOLATE COVERED STRAWBERRIES

Yield: 4 servings | Prep time: 15 minutes | Cook time: 5 minutes

Ingredients:

16 large strawberries, washed and dried 2 teaspoons coconut oil	8 ounces dark chocolate, chopped	Optional toppings: crushed nuts, shredded coconut, or sea salt

Directions:

1. Line a baking sheet with parchment paper. In a microwave-safe bowl, combine dark chocolate and coconut oil. Microwave in 30-second intervals, stirring between each, until the chocolate is completely melted and smooth.

2. Hold a strawberry by the stem and dip it into the melted chocolate, twisting slightly to let the excess chocolate drip off. Place the strawberry on the prepared baking sheet. Repeat with the remaining strawberries.

3. If using, sprinkle your chosen toppings over the strawberries before the chocolate sets.

4. Place the baking sheet in the refrigerator for at least 30 minutes to allow the chocolate to harden.

Nutritional information. Per serving: calories: 220, protein: 3g, carbohydrates: 26g, fat: 14g, fiber: 4g, cholesterol: 0mg, sodium: 20mg, potassium: 340mg.

Dark Chocolate Covered Strawberries are a luxurious yet simple treat that combines the sweetness of ripe strawberries with the rich bitterness of dark chocolate. This elegant dessert is perfect for special occasions or as a decadent snack. The addition of coconut oil gives the chocolate a glossy finish and makes it easier to work with, while optional toppings like crushed nuts or sea salt can add an extra layer of flavor and texture.

AVOCADO CHOCOLATE MOUSSE

Yield: 4 servings | Prep time: 15 minutes | Cook time: 0 minutes

Ingredients:

2 ripe avocados, peeled and pitted 1/4 cup unsweetened cocoa powder	1/4 cup honey or maple syrup 1/2 teaspoon vanilla extract	1 pinch of salt 1/4 cup almond milk or milk of choice, adjust as needed for texture

Directions:

1. Place the avocados, cocoa powder, honey (or maple syrup), vanilla extract, and a pinch of salt in a blender or food processor. Blend until the mixture is smooth and creamy.

2. Gradually add the almond milk until you reach your desired consistency for the mousse. Blend well to incorporate all the ingredients evenly.

3. Taste and adjust the sweetness if necessary by adding a little more honey or maple syrup.

4. Divide the mousse into serving dishes and refrigerate for at least 1 hour to chill and set.

5. Serve chilled, optionally garnished with fresh berries, whipped cream, or a sprinkle of cocoa powder.

Nutritional information. Per serving: calories: 240, protein: 3g, carbohydrates: 27g, fat: 15g, fiber: 7g, cholesterol: 0mg, sodium: 60mg, potassium: 487mg.

This Avocado Chocolate Mousse is a rich, creamy, and healthy alternative to traditional chocolate mousse. Made with ripe avocados, it offers a perfect blend of natural fats, fibers, and nutrients, making it an indulgent yet guilt-free dessert. Its smooth texture and deep chocolate flavor are sure to satisfy any sweet tooth, while also providing beneficial antioxidants and vitamins.

NO-SUGAR-ADDED PEACH COBBLER WITH ALMOND FLOUR TOPPING

Yield: 4 servings | Prep time: 15 minutes | Cook time: 35 minutes

Ingredients:

For the Filling:	1/4 teaspoon nutmeg	1/4 cup unsalted butter, melted
4 cups sliced fresh peaches (about 4-5 medium peaches)	2 tablespoons water	1 teaspoon vanilla extract
1 tablespoon lemon juice	For the Topping:	1/2 teaspoon baking powder
1 teaspoon cinnamon	1 cup almond flour	1/4 teaspoon salt
	1 egg	

Directions:

1. Preheat the oven to 375°F (190°C). In a large bowl, toss the sliced peaches with lemon juice, cinnamon, nutmeg, and water. Transfer the mixture to a 9-inch pie dish or baking dish.

2. In a separate bowl, mix together the almond flour, melted butter, egg, vanilla extract, baking powder, and salt until a dough forms. Crumble the dough evenly over the peach filling.

3. Bake in the preheated oven for about 35 minutes, or until the topping is golden brown and the peach filling is bubbly.

4. Let the cobbler cool slightly before serving. It can be served warm or at room temperature, optionally with a dollop of whipped cream or a scoop of sugar-free ice cream.

Nutritional information. Per serving: calories: 320, protein: 8g, carbohydrates: 24g, fat: 24g, fiber: 6g, cholesterol: 70mg, sodium: 160mg, potassium: 400mg.

This No-Sugar-Added Peach Cobbler with Almond Flour Topping offers a health-conscious twist on the classic Southern dessert, perfect for those monitoring their sugar intake. The natural sweetness of ripe peaches, combined with the nutty, buttery topping, creates a satisfying dessert that doesn't skimp on flavor. Enjoy the warm, comforting taste of peach cobbler without the added sugar, making it a guilt-free pleasure for any occasion.

COCONUT FLOUR CHOCOLATE CHIP COOKIES

Yield: 4 servings | Prep time: 10 minutes | Cook time: 12 minutes

Ingredients:

1/2 cup coconut flour 1/4 cup unsalted butter, melted 2 large eggs	1/4 cup pure maple syrup or honey 1/2 teaspoon vanilla extract	1/4 teaspoon salt 1/2 teaspoon baking soda 1/2 cup dark chocolate chips

Directions:

1. Preheat the oven to 350°F (175°C) and line a baking sheet with parchment paper.
2. In a large bowl, combine the coconut flour, melted butter, maple syrup (or honey), eggs, vanilla extract, salt, and baking soda. Mix until well combined.
3. Fold in the chocolate chips until evenly distributed throughout the batter.
4. Scoop tablespoon-sized amounts of the dough onto the prepared baking sheet, spacing them about 2 inches apart. Flatten slightly with the back of the spoon.
5. Bake for 10-12 minutes, or until the edges are golden brown. Allow the cookies to cool on the baking sheet for a few minutes before transferring them to a wire rack to cool completely.

Nutritional information. Per serving: calories: 280, protein: 5g, carbohydrates: 24g, fat: 18g, fiber: 6g, cholesterol: 105mg, sodium: 220mg, potassium: 100mg.

These Coconut Flour Chocolate Chip Cookies are a delightful twist on the classic treat, perfect for those looking for a gluten-free or lower-carb option. The coconut flour provides a subtle sweetness and soft texture, while the dark chocolate chips add richness. Enjoy these cookies as a guilt-free dessert or a tasty snack anytime.

GREEK YOGURT PARFAIT WITH NUTS AND BERRIES

Yield: 4 servings | Prep time: 10 minutes | Cook time: 0 minutes

Ingredients:

2 cups Greek yogurt, unsweetened 1/2 cup nuts (almonds, walnuts), chopped	1 cup mixed berries (strawberries, blueberries, raspberries)	2 tablespoons chia seeds 1 teaspoon vanilla extract Optional: Stevia or monk fruit sweetener to taste

Directions:

1. In a bowl, mix the Greek yogurt with vanilla extract and a sweetener of your choice (if using) until well combined.

2. Take four glasses or parfait cups. Layer the Greek yogurt mixture, mixed berries, and nuts alternatively in the cups. Start with a layer of yogurt, then a layer of berries, and a sprinkle of nuts.

3. Repeat the layering process until all ingredients are used up, finishing with a layer of berries and nuts on top.

4. Sprinkle the top of each parfait with chia seeds for an extra boost of fiber and omega-3 fatty acids.

Nutritional Information. Per serving: 220 calories, 20g protein, 18g carbohydrates, 10g fat, 5g fiber, 10mg cholesterol, 60mg sodium, 300mg potassium.

This Greek Yogurt Parfait with Nuts and Berries is a delightful and nutritious option for anyone managing diabetes. It's packed with protein from the Greek yogurt, antioxidants from the berries, healthy fats from the nuts, and fiber from the chia seeds, making it a balanced and satisfying breakfast or snack. The use of unsweetened yogurt and optional natural sweeteners ensures it's low in added sugars, perfectly aligning with a diabetic-friendly diet.

14. DRINKS

BERRY BLAST SMOOTHIE

Yield: 4 servings | Prep time: 5 minutes | Cook time: 0 minutes

Ingredients

2 cups mixed berries (strawberries, blueberries, raspberries), fresh or frozen 1 cup unsweetened almond milk	1 cup Greek yogurt, low-fat 2 tablespoons chia seeds 2 tablespoons flaxseed meal 1 teaspoon vanilla extract	1 tablespoon sugar substitute (suitable for diabetics, like stevia) Ice cubes (optional, if using fresh berries)

Directions

1. Place the mixed berries, unsweetened almond milk, Greek yogurt, chia seeds, flaxseed meal, sugar substitute, and vanilla extract in a blender.

2. Blend on high until smooth. If the mixture is too thick, you can add a little more almond milk to reach your desired consistency.

3. If using fresh berries and you prefer a colder smoothie, add a handful of ice cubes and blend again until smooth.

4. Serve immediately, garnished with a few whole berries on top if desired.

Nutritional Information. Per serving: 150 calories, 10g protein, 18g carbohydrates, 5g fat, 6g fiber, 5mg cholesterol, 80mg sodium, 250mg potassium.

This Berry Blast Smoothie offers a refreshing, nutritious option for diabetics, focusing on high fiber, antioxidants, and protein while keeping the sugar content low. The use of a sugar substitute and unsweetened almond milk helps maintain blood sugar levels, making it an ideal choice for a healthy breakfast or snack.

GOLDEN MILK

Yield: 2 servings | Prep time: 5 minutes | Cook time: 10 minutes

Ingredients

2 cups almond milk (unsweetened)	1/2 teaspoon ground cinnamon	1 tablespoon honey or sugar substitute (suitable for diabetics, like stevia)
1 tablespoon turmeric	1/4 teaspoon ground ginger	
1 tablespoon coconut oil		A pinch of black pepper

Directions

1. In a small saucepan, whisk together almond milk, turmeric, cinnamon, ginger, and black pepper over medium heat. Ensure the mixture is well combined and there are no lumps.

2. Add coconut oil and honey or sugar substitute to the saucepan. Whisk continuously for about 10 minutes on medium heat, but do not allow the mixture to come to a boil.

3. Once heated through and fully mixed, remove from heat. Taste and adjust sweetness or spices as desired.

4. Serve warm, dividing the mixture between two mugs.

Nutritional Information. Per serving: 150 calories, 2g protein, 8g carbohydrates, 12g fat, 1g fiber, 0mg cholesterol, 120mg sodium, 50mg potassium.

Golden Milk, with its main ingredient turmeric, is celebrated for its anti-inflammatory and antioxidant properties. This recipe, adapted for the US market, uses ingredients like almond milk and coconut oil to cater to dietary preferences and health-conscious individuals, including those managing diabetes. The addition of a sugar substitute instead of honey can help maintain blood sugar levels, making it a comforting and healthy drink option.

GREEN SMOOTHIE

Yield: 4 servings | Prep time: 5 minutes | Cook time: 0 minutes

Ingredients

2 cups fresh spinach 2 cups unsweetened almond milk	2 ripe bananas, peeled 1 apple, cored and sliced 1/2 avocado	2 tablespoons flaxseeds Ice cubes (optional, for a colder smoothie)

Directions

1. Add the spinach and almond milk to a blender and blend until smooth, ensuring no spinach leaves are left whole.

2. Add the bananas, apple, avocado, and flaxseeds to the blender. If you prefer a colder smoothie, add ice cubes as desired.

3. Blend on high until the smoothie reaches your desired consistency, adding more almond milk if it's too thick.

4. Taste and adjust the sweetness if necessary, although the natural sweetness from the fruits usually suffices.

5. Serve immediately, pouring the smoothie into the glasses.

Nutritional Information. Per serving: 190 calories, 4g protein, 27g carbohydrates, 9g fat, 7g fiber, 0mg cholesterol, 95mg sodium, 600mg potassium.

This Green Smoothie recipe is a nutrient-dense drink that combines the goodness of leafy greens, fruits, and healthy fats, making it suitable for the US market, especially for those seeking healthful, energizing beverage options. The inclusion of flaxseeds adds omega-3 fatty acids and fiber, contributing to the smoothie's nutritional value and making it a great option for a quick breakfast or a refreshing snack.

GINGER LEMONADE

Yield: 4 servings | Prep time: 10 minutes | Cook time: 0 minutes

Ingredients

4 cups water 1/2 cup fresh lemon juice (about 2-3 large lemons) Ice cubes	1/3 cup honey or sugar substitute (suitable for diabetics, like stevia equivalent)	2 tablespoons fresh ginger, grated Lemon slices and mint leaves for garnish

Directions

1. In a small saucepan, combine 1 cup of water with the honey (or sugar substitute) and grated ginger. Heat over medium heat, stirring until the honey is dissolved completely. Remove from heat and allow it to cool to room temperature. This creates a ginger-infused syrup.

2. Strain the ginger syrup to remove the ginger pieces, and pour it into a large pitcher.

3. Add the fresh lemon juice and the remaining 3 cups of water to the pitcher. Stir well to combine.

4. Refrigerate until chilled. Serve over ice, garnished with lemon slices and mint leaves.

Nutritional Information. Per serving: 60 calories, 0g protein, 17g carbohydrates, 0g fat, 0g fiber, 0mg cholesterol, 10mg sodium, 50mg potassium.

Ginger Lemonade offers a refreshing twist on traditional lemonade, with the added health benefits of ginger, known for its anti-inflammatory properties. This recipe uses a honey or sugar substitute to sweeten the drink, making it suitable for those monitoring their sugar intake, including diabetics. The result is a thirst-quenching, low-calorie beverage perfect for hot summer days or as a healthful everyday drink.

TURMERIC LATTE

Yield: 2 servings | Prep time: 5 minutes | Cook time: 5 minutes

Ingredients

2 cups almond milk (unsweetened) 1 teaspoon turmeric powder 1/2 teaspoon cinnamon powder	1/4 teaspoon ginger powder 1 tablespoon honey or sugar substitute (suitable for diabetics, like stevia)	A pinch of black pepper (to enhance turmeric absorption) 1 teaspoon vanilla extract

Directions

1. In a small saucepan, heat the almond milk over medium heat until it is warm but not boiling.

2. Whisk in the turmeric, cinnamon, ginger, black pepper, and vanilla extract until well combined.

3. Remove from heat and stir in the honey or sugar substitute, adjusting the amount to taste.

4. Divide the mixture between two mugs, using a frother to froth the top if desired.

5. Serve immediately, optionally garnished with a sprinkle of cinnamon on top.

Nutritional Information. Per serving: 90 calories, 1g protein, 9g carbohydrates, 4g fat, 1g fiber, 0mg cholesterol, 150mg sodium, 200mg potassium.

This Turmeric Latte, also known as "Golden Milk," is a warming, nutritious drink that's gaining popularity in the US for its health benefits, including anti-inflammatory properties. This version uses almond milk and a sugar substitute to make it suitable for diabetics, ensuring a low-calorie, heart-healthy option that fits well into a variety of dietary needs.

SPARKLING WATER WITH CITRUS AND FRESH HERBS

Yield: 4 servings | Prep time: 5 minutes | Cook time: 0 minutes

Ingredients

4 cups chilled sparkling water 1/2 lemon, thinly sliced 1/2 lime, thinly sliced 1/2 orange, thinly sliced	1/4 cup fresh mint leaves, gently torn to release their oils 1/4 cup fresh basil leaves, gently torn	Ice cubes, as needed Optional: 1 tablespoon of honey or a suitable sugar substitute for a hint of sweetness

Directions

1. In a large pitcher, combine the sliced lemon, lime, and orange. Add the fresh mint and basil leaves. If using honey or a sugar substitute, add it to the pitcher now.

2. Gently muddle the mixture with a spoon or a muddler to release the citrus juices and the essential oils from the mint and basil leaves, being careful not to break apart the fruit completely.

3. Fill the pitcher with ice cubes to about halfway, then pour the chilled sparkling water over the top. Stir gently to combine, allowing the flavors to meld together.

4. Serve the sparkling water in individual glasses, ensuring that each glass gets a good mix of citrus slices and fresh herbs. Add more ice if desired.

5. Garnish with additional mint or basil leaves for a decorative touch and an extra burst of freshness.

Nutritional Information. Per serving: 10 calories, 0g protein, 3g carbohydrates, 0g fat, 0g fiber, 0mg cholesterol, 5mg sodium, 20mg potassium.

This Sparkling Water with Citrus and Fresh Herbs recipe is a delightful, refreshing drink that's perfect for any occasion, from a casual gathering to a festive celebration. The infusion of fresh citrus and herbs not only adds a vibrant flavor but also provides a visually appealing presentation. With virtually no calories and no added sugars (unless you opt for a touch of honey or a sugar substitute), it's an ideal choice for those looking for a healthy, hydrating option that's both delicious and sophisticated.

CUCUMBER MINT COOLER

Yield: 4 servings | Prep time: 10 minutes | Cook time: 0 minutes

Ingredients

2 large cucumbers, peeled and chopped 1/4 cup fresh mint leaves 2 tablespoons lime juice	2 tablespoons honey or sugar substitute (suitable for diabetics, like stevia) 4 cups cold water	Ice cubes Additional cucumber slices and mint leaves for garnish

Directions

1. In a blender, combine the chopped cucumbers, mint leaves, lime juice, and honey or sugar substitute. Blend until smooth.

2. Pour the mixture through a fine mesh strainer into a large pitcher, pressing on the solids to extract as much liquid as possible. Discard the solids.

3. Add cold water to the cucumber mixture in the pitcher. Stir well to combine.

4. Serve the cooler over ice, garnished with additional cucumber slices and mint leaves.

Nutritional Information. Per serving: 50 calories, 0g protein, 12g carbohydrates, 0g fat, 1g fiber, 0mg cholesterol, 10mg sodium, 150mg potassium.

This Cucumber Mint Cooler is a refreshing, hydrating drink perfect for warm weather or after workouts. Its low-calorie profile and the use of a sugar substitute make it suitable for diabetics and those monitoring their sugar intake. The cucumber and mint offer a fresh, light flavor, while the lime juice adds a zesty kick.

CONCLUSIONS AND WISHES

As we bring the pages of this cookbook to a close, I hope that you, the reader, have found a new sense of empowerment and inspiration in your journey towards managing diabetes. The book "Diabetic Cookbook for Beginners: Simple and Delicious Recipes for Type 2, Prediabetes, and Newly Diagnosed Diabetes" was crafted with a singular vision: to provide you with the tools and knowledge to master your health through delicious, low-carb, and low-sugar meals.

Embarking on this journey, we began with an essential understanding of diabetes, navigating through the complexities of nutrition recommendations tailored for a diabetic-friendly diet. Each recipe, from the comforting warmth of Blueberry Almond Oatmeal to the savory depths of Beef Bourguignon and the refreshing simplicity of Berry Blast Smoothies, was designed not only to nourish but also to delight your palate while keeping your health in check.

I aimed to demystify the idea that a diabetes diagnosis means the end of enjoying food. Instead, I've shown that it can be the beginning of a new, healthful, and flavorful culinary adventure. These recipes serve as a foundation upon which you can build, experiment, and personalize, making each dish a testament to your journey toward a healthier lifestyle.

As you continue to explore and experiment with these recipes, remember that managing diabetes is a journey, not a destination. It's about making informed choices, understanding your body's needs, and finding joy in the meals you create. Let this cookbook be a constant companion in your kitchen, a source of inspiration when you seek it, and a reminder that your health is worth every bite.

Thank you for allowing me to be a part of your journey. Here's to many more delicious and healthful meals ahead.

With warmest wishes for your health and happiness,

Andrew Forestry

ABOUT THE AUTHOR
Meet the Author: Andrew Forestry

Expert. As a seasoned culinary expert and devoted diabetes advocate, Andrew Forestry is on a mission to empower individuals to embrace a healthy and delicious lifestyle, even in the face of diabetes. With years of experience in crafting mouthwatering recipes tailored for type 2 diabetes, prediabetes, and the newly diagnosed, Andrew Forestry understands the unique challenges individuals face. His approach combines culinary creativity with a deep understanding of nutritional needs.

Health and Wellness Advocate. Andrew Forestry is not just a cookbook author; she/he is a champion for health and wellness. Through her/his books, Andrew Forestry strives to make nutritious and delectable meals accessible to everyone, promoting a positive impact on overall well-being.

Simple and Delicious Recipes. In Andrew Forestry's "Diabetic Cookbook for Beginners: simple and delicious recipes for Type 2, prediabetes, and newly diagnosed diabetes. Master Your Health with Delicious Low-Carb and Low-Sugar Meals" savor the fruits of her/his culinary expertise. Every recipe is a testament to Andrew Forestry's commitment to making healthy eating an enjoyable journey.

Stay Current with 2024's Latest Culinary Trends. Andrew Forestry doesn't just stop at recipes; he ensures that the last edition is a reflection of the latest culinary trends and nutritional knowledge. Stay ahead with Andrew Forestry's innovative approach to diabetes-friendly cooking.

Made in the USA
Coppell, TX
10 April 2024

31144670R00083